Black coral is exotic and rare,
most precious in color above all other varieties of coral.

Black Coral: A Daughter's Apology to Her Asian Island Mother

This story, a personal saga, carries a powerful message about race and class in contemporary America, and the interplay of the two, as they percolated in the post World War II era to the present. It is about complex family dynamics, a mix of cultures, the long-lasting effects that one's family can have on a child, racial identity formation and self esteem, and the importance of perceiving a mother's love.

The timing for the telling of this story is right. While Cheryl Holmes Miller's journey began in the 1950's, the message is more powerful and important today than it would have been if told earlier. Our understanding of bi-raciality today, a departure from the reductionist "one drop rule" of past eras, speaks to the reality of identity for more and more Americans. Sociologically, the book challenges the meaning of race in the 21st century as it continues to become even more multifaceted and permeated.

Today, many say race does not matter. Today, many say they don't see color/race. Today, many say children do not perceive race differences. Cheryl Holmes Miller's story shows the reader how America's inability to grapple successfully with race and difference colored her childhood years in ways that were wounding, tumultuous, and profound.

Her journey reflects the confluence of both lineage and experience in shaping the person. It attests to the twists and turns of the nuances of racial identity formation, and the importance of developing a strong and clear racial identity and pride. Problems herein create family tensions, emotional uncertainty, diminished self esteem and a false sense of self and one's place in the world, all of which, as Miller's story attests, are difficult from which to heal.

Black Coral is a must read for bi-racial families, and scholars of race and class. It is an illuminating ethnography of the complexities of bi-raciality, the meaning of race, and racial identity formation. It speaks to the complexity of the issue of race today, and exemplifies the spoils of America's inability to grapple well with definitions of the concept and indeed with race itself.

Susan D. Toliver, PhD, CFLE
Professor and Chair
Department of Sociology
Iona College

Black Coral: A Daughter's Apology to Her Asian Island Mother is a whirlwind journey that bravely and honestly walks down several exciting paths simultaneously, with each path being unreservedly too familiar with second generation Filipinos living in the United States. Thoughtfully written, each chapter adds another layer that shines more light on the inspiring life of C.D. Holmes Miller.

Many Filipinos raised in the United States struggle with their identity in relation to their family's native country, the Philippines. *Black Coral* not only serves as a record of one mixed-raced Filipina American's experience, but as testimony that proactively connecting with your roots in the Philippines can be one of the most fulfilling experiences of your life; and that starting your journey toward that self-actualization is never too late. Miller's half Filipina mother, abandoned post WWI and immigrating from the U.S. Virgin Islands rather than the Philippines is a story which speaks to the many bi-racial and mixed race Filipinos in America whose struggle with their own ethnic identity becomes exponentially more trying within the backdrop of being raised as an American first and a Filipino last. *Black Coral* serves as a great addition to the evolving Filipino American narrative.

Steven Raga, MPP

Board of Trustees, Pilipino American Unity for Progress (UniPro)

National Chairman, Filipino American Civic Engagement (FACE)

Black Coral: A great deal has been written about Washington D.C., but very rarely does the reader see a glimpse of the rarefied atmosphere of the Black Bourgeosie of the 1950's and 1960's. This world of the African-American "elite," with its august social clubs was an important part of Washington, but a difficult one in which to gain a foothold. Reverend Miller's search for who she is, a mixed child of an up-and-coming black leader and his demure Filipino Caribbean wife who had her own difficulty fitting in, was intriguing both on a personal, sociological, and spiritual level. It truly hit home as someone who survived these times in Washington, but moreover as someone for whom "fitting in" has been a life struggle.

As I started reading about her voyage through her "green box" of memories, I was both enthralled and excited. She discovered answers to her lifelong questions. Through her personal journey, she has given us a path to follow toward our individual healing.

Her book brought out personal memories of these times and allowed me to see not only who she is, but also who I am. As I moved through her story, excited to find out the newest discovery in her amazing faith walk, I realized that her journey was my journey.

Judith Mann Walk

Native Washingtonian, Director of Admissions,

Howard University College of Medicine

BLACK CORAL

A DAUGHTER'S APOLOGY TO HER ASIAN ISLAND MOTHER

C.D. HOLMES MILLER

AAGE HERITAGE PRESS
CONNECTICUT

Published by

Aage Heritage Press

http://aageheritagepress.com, http://cdholmesmiller.com,
http://blackcoralthebook.com

Imprint of BCDM, LLC. Publishers

Quoted verses of scriptures
The Holy Bible, King James Version
All photos are with permission from the family collections, C.D. Holmes-Miller
Cover and Typography Design by- C.D. Holmes-Miller
Pagination Layout by- Theresa P. Allen
Mangyan Treasures with permission by- Mangyan Heritage Center, Inc.
Antoon Postma, 2005
Oriental Mindoro, Philippines

ISBN: 9780989263207
ISBN: 9780989263214 - ebook
Library of Congress Control Number
LCCN: 2013909120

Printed in the United States of America.

To Momma–

I had a chance to share my love

with everyone else, except you–

I give you the love you always deserved.

Norma Sabino Holmes Weston
"Normsie"

Hanunuo Mangyan Ambahan from

Mangyan Treasures by Antoon Postma

Says the baby, lifeless born:
My beloved mother dear,
Father, oh, my father dear.
When still resting in your womb,
Closely united with you,
I was father's favorite.
Taken from my safe abode,
placed upon the bamboo floor,
no one put me on your lap,
no one rocked me in a crib.
What became my crib at last,
was a hammock strongly built:
as a bed, a burial hill.
Discarded I was, unloved.
Covering me was the cold earth
and the weeping sky above.
But although it be like this,
a happier day will come.
Maybe it'll be coming soon.
And what will be happening then?
The old people weeping, sad,
in a darkening, mourning sky:
I will finally leave behind.

TABLE OF CONTENTS

ACKNOWLEDGEMENTS

I have been on an odyssey to destiny. A 20 year historical, sociological, and genealogical fact finding journey has given me an incredible story to share. I thank the Lord Jesus Christ for inviting me on a voyage to receive truth I was not looking for. May my husband Phillip remain on the top list of those whom I eternally thank for loving and caring for me. My answered prayer of having a little brother, Horace, Jr., Chico, has been my greatest joy. My precious children have shared me to the endless hours necessary for writing my story. Many thanks to friends and family who know my words to this incredible saga to be absolutely true.

Family historians and researchers have been called to my rescue. They have offered hope, knowledge, facts and photos to inform me of my family heritage. I thank Eliseo Basa, Ellis Collins, Susan Cote, Pedrito Francois, Aimery Caron, Cheryl Fuller and Gaines- Holmes family historians, Angel Bernardo Guinto, Lori Guinto, Bishop Kent T. Holmes, Mary Holmes, Karen Hughes White, June Jackson, Leona Romeo-Martin, Gener Marquez, Marlene McEnheimer, Victoria O'Flaherty, David M. Pemberton, Arman Sabino, Debbie Sabino, Tommy Sabino, V. Chapman-Smith, Larry Sewer, Mattie Taylor, Earl Toliver, Lisa Tyler, Wayne Webster,

Jerri Williams and The William Strother Organization. I thank our published reviewers: Dr. James A. Forbes, Jr., Steven Raga, Dr. Susan Toliver, Rob Upson, and Judith Walk for their critical reflections. The greatest friend who has given me her best gift is Carole Hall. Carole, I thank you for the years of walking the steps of this story with me. Thank you very much. This story is told thanks to your love of literature, storytelling, editorial excellence and me. Your unconditional listening has helped to heal my heart. May God bless you in the receiving the desires of your heart.

I thank my dear friends Mercedes Anderson, Sheryl Battles, Sheila Foster, Kit Hughes, Rita Jackson, Susan Johnson, Alfred Prettyman, Rita Robles and Ann Williams for patiently listening to my story countless times as if listening for the first time, every time.

Peter Hildick-Smith you are such a gift. Peter thank you for your marketing reality checks. Thank you very much to Will Powell, my developmental editor. Will, you helped me to obey Carole's advice, "Say it once and take the air out of the story." Thank you Ryan Holden for assistance with copyediting.

I pray dearly for the 52,000 Filipino Amerasians who have been abandoned in the Philippines by American Soldiers from WWII to 1992. I acknowledge you; I love you. I may not have shared the hardship but I know the pain, intimately. You have come into my life to let me know, I am not alone. Thank you for waiting to read *Black Coral.*

FOREWORD

I write the foreword to this book with deep pride and satisfaction. It was my pleasure to work closely with the author of this self-revealing, truth disclosing and hope inspiring "journal of a journey into wholeness." I stood by and observed her wrestling with the unresolved conflict of which she writes and I share the delight to see the confirmation of the truth that "all things work together for good to those who love God." The title of her book *Black Coral* speaks of rare beauty which grows in the luminous darkness of deep and hidden special places. Through the twenty years of her quest she learned to embrace the truth that love of self and others may not always come from brightly lit pathways but sometimes through the valley of the shadow of death. The complicating dynamic which is the theme of this work touches the occupants of the White House on 1600 Pennsylvania Avenue and a family raised in a red brick house a few miles up 16th Street in Washington D.C. The struggle to be fully oneself is a Herculean task, but if one makes it through to the finish line, it will be worth all the blood, sweat and tears. One woman's story intersects with the meandering paths we all travel to find our way home to ourselves. Consider the fact that Barack Obama, C.D. Holmes Miller and increasing numbers of global citizens share the gift and possible burden of multi-racial ancestry. This testimony of trial and triumph may help to convince us that our varied genetic ingredients are gifts toward a beautiful blend rather than an awful burden we have to bear.

After the inauguration of Barack Obama as the 44th President of the United States of America there was talk of our having become a post-racial society. It was not long after the Obamas moved into the White House that it became clear to everyone that race is alive and continues to assert itself into the dynamics of the social, economic and political climate in our nation.

We speak of having our first African~American president, but the truth, which we have not quite engaged in serious public discourse, is that Mr. Obama is the son of mixed-race parentage. What does this mean in terms of his identity, his leadership approach and his racial~ethnic sensitivities? Does our social milieu make it possible for him to rise above identity politics? Are relatives from either side of his ancestral origins willing to let him be all of who he is and to honor the blackness and whiteness which courses through his body with each heartbeat? Will the "one-drop-of-black-blood" formula disenfranchise or cancel the strength derived from whatever was the unique genetic and environmental input from a different genome or geography?

Carlyle Marney once told me, "No man (or woman) amounts to much unless he (or she) is able to bless his (or her) own origins." Despite widespread denial about the polarizing impact of race the

Obama presidency has already started to pull the blinders from our eyes about the destructive consequences of racism and its malignant manifestations. Will we see the peril of our racially infested past soon enough to turn toward a future enriched by the blessing of the freedom to be one family under God?

In *Black Coral*, C.D. Holmes Miller shares her story of what happens when ones personhood is sliced and diced on account of racial ideology and ethnic quarantine. While cleaning out the basement of the house of her childhood she discovers a "green box" of records and vital data containing soul-wrenching details of the struggle of her Filipina Amerasian West Indian mother whose love for and marriage to a black man required her to fit the racial categories of the census bureau. The loved child of that relationship is the author-confessor of this heart-breaking story. Miller's account tells some truth about all of us who live in a culture where race keeps on insinuating its compartmentalizing control over who can be family, friends, neighbors or co-workers. Race not only splits her larger family, but in an almost demonic way makes it impossible for her to accept her mother. She had chosen to be a black princess in the D.C. black bourgeoisie. This, she assumes, will require an authentic looking black woman to raise her into proper womanhood. By the time she opens the "green box" and understands for the first time the diabolical barriers race had erected between mother and daughter, her mother had died. And it was, in a sense, too late to do anything about it.

She had lost something that could never be retrieved. She grieved and lamented what this "mixed-race thing" had done to her. A perfect storm of rationalizations and justifications immobilized all the systems of her self-condemning soul. Somehow, by mercy and grace, she summoned the strength to resume and complete the torturous genealogical odyssey. Was it the arrival of another multi-racial man at the other end of 16th Street that catalyzed her readiness to pick up the pieces and forge ahead? Maybe. Perhaps not. Nevertheless she found herself declaring unapologetic acceptance of every jot and tittle of her being -- biological, sociological, psychological and spiritual.

The story reads like a novel but it is a true and documented autobiographical account of what happened in spite of racial and, ethnic interference. Reverend Miller does not preach here, but one would have to put on blinders not to see some truth she hopes will make its own case. I dare not spoil your enjoyment of this enthralling interplay of agony and ecstasy by disclosing too much of the story, but allow me to suggest some questions that may be worth asking along the way: Has race overplayed its hand in your life? Do its imagined benefits deliver enough of what it promises to make it worth the deficits? How does one break out of its stranglehold to enjoy the richness of not having to put people into boxes? What would it be like to live in either a post-racial society or a society where diversity and difference make all of us philanthropists to each other when we find the courage to be who we are?

Are you willing to allow your folks to forgive people who have been in bondage to bias, bigotry and tribalistic systems of oppression and to join you and them in becoming human race activists?

Rev. Dr. James A. Forbes, Jr.
Harry Emerson Fosdick Distinguished Professor
Union Theological Seminary of New York City
Senior Minister Emeritus, The Riverside Church, New York, N.Y.
Healing of the Nations Foundation, President and Founder

The Green Box of vital records contained a true story which had to be revealed.

INTRODUCTION

Since I was always thinking about the "me" of my story, I never really thought about Momma's point of view. I must have embarrassed her. Momma was married to my father, a 1950s Washington, D.C. Head-Negro-in-Charge, and behind that perfect picture was me, just as crazy as a firecracker lit on both ends.

As a black, prominent, Northwest Washington, D.C. uptown family, we presented ourselves well, but our "mark-of-excellence" house was not always a home. We were a multiracial, multiethnic family aspiring as black folks in a 1950s America, so we had issues. We had severe interfamily racial drama, actually.

In the 1959 movie *Imitation of Life,* mulatto daughter Sarah Jane cried out, in spite of her black mammy-like mother, "I'm somebody else. I'm white...white... WHITE." In 1959, I cried out, "I'm black, I'm black, I'm BLACK," in spite of my Filipina-Danish West Indian mother. I just wanted to be a popular little black girl with a fun-loving black mother and a successful black daddy, but that isn't quite what I had.

I have lived a real Fannie Hurst, *Imitation of Life bangungot*—a silent nightmare. When I first saw this tear-jerker as a child, I knew it would be my fate. I knew that I would hang over my mother's coffin and express my love for her, but it would be too late. I can't describe the heartache that has brought me. Momma was beautiful and exotic. In my childhood world, to have this particular type of woman as a mother made me very odd. Besides being hard to explain to my circle of black bourgeoisie friends, Momma was a foreigner from somewhere different, who spoke different, appeared different, and behaved different from everyone else. There is no other way to describe the situation, other than just *different*. I was dissatisfied with my "Asian Island" Momma who didn't understand her own uniqueness as it related to American racial values, and this made me dissatisfied with myself.

"Cher'rell, you are always thinking of yourself," she would contend. The honest-to-God's truth is that as a child, I punished Momma with rude behavior and a smart mouth for making me an outcast. With every opportunity, I made her life miserable for making mine unbearable. After all, I was a black child with a funny kind of mother.

If she was peculiar, so was I.

"Cheryl, just be the best black woman you can be," my father told me as a solution, and believe me, I have become a very blessed woman as a result. I have not one reason to complain, but trust me when I tell you that what happened to all of us was just a shame. My story is about life's most precious unit—family, and everything a family shouldn't do if they find themselves having to racially and culturally blend in to being happy as a family. As we change the color palette of America, don't let your family become suffocated by "one-drop, one-box" thinking like mine was.

The entire situation is what Momma called a "roo goo do" i.e., the Virgin Island creole phrase for a messed up, confused situation. We lived a life full of mysteries and lots of them, at that.

Momma's mystery race, ethnicity and culture had nothing to do with me, so I thought. "The Green Box came to speak of its truth."... C.D. Holmes Miller

PART I

"Can a woman forget her sucking child, that she should not

have compassion on the child of her womb?

Yea, they may forget, yet will I not forget thee."

–Isaiah 49:15

THE MAGENS BAY REVELATION

Momma's health suffered after Poppa's death. Although I thought it was attention-getting behavior at the time, I now think a lifetime of disappointment was the source of her ailments. Poppa died at 44 and she became a young widow, left in his strange land with black teenagers. Way down deep, where the soul cries, Momma had been traumatized by Poppa's fatal illness, and I don't think she ever recovered.

Ultimately, her broken heart and our rocky road together gave way to chronic renal disease. In her elderly years, she needed tri-weekly dialysis treatments, had two in-remission bouts with cancer, and experienced constant back pain. Since I was living far away from Washington, D.C, all I could do was call her on a regular basis.

"Momma, how are you ma'an (man or mon)," I asked her during a call in 2000.

"Ma'an, I wish I could find my faddah, maybe I could understand why I am always so sick. Maybe it's in our family health history. Ma'an, dis back 'ting, Cher'rell, I am going to the pain management center at the hospital. Ma'an, I remember, I just married ya faddah, and was a registered nurse at D.C. General Hospital. I fell one night on the way to work, and we had a mid-Atlantic winter's snow storm. I tripped in front of the hospital and landed on my back.

Ma'an, I hurt my spine and never really treated da 'ting. I've lived with it. Da 'ting caught up with me and it developed into a degenerated disc ailment. My bones are rubbin' together. Dey gave me a back pain patch. Dealin' wit it ma'an," Momma said.

"Momma, can't they do anything else for you?"

John, my stepfather, loved and cared for Momma in her final days. I will always appreciate him for that, whereas all I could do was pray for her.

Sometimes, I think Momma believed in a little *obeah,* an island, Voodoo-like belief, about her first child being a girl. You have "good man luck" if your first born was a male child, and Lawdy, there was no telling what you would get if your womb was opened by a female baby. Momma believed in this *obeah* curse called "gout mout" or "goat mouth," which was a prophetic threat, certain to pass.

"Ma'an, you dun't wan me to put my mout on ya, meh'son," she would threaten, and I'd heard it a thousand times. "Y'are gonna miss me when I am gone. You dun't miss your water until your well runs dry."

"I am the child and you are the mother. How did you let this happen to us?"

"You are going to kill me with that mouth of yours. You gonna miss me when I gone, ma'an. You tried to kill me once when I was pregnant with you; I was so sick."

I did not see how in the world I would ever miss this mixed race, mother-daughter nightmare. It seemed as if her death, which wasn't far away, was the only way out of it all. My arguments with Momma became more severe.

Once, while visiting my maternal family in the U.S. Virgin Islands, I joined a dawn swim at Magens Bay Beach like all the St. Thomas island locals do before tourists and cruise ships arrive in the morning. I know the island way, I have a home there, and I can speak with a little accent when I need to. I get my native island birth rights from Momma. I am one of "Sabino's own," Sabino being my maternal family's Filipino surname. Everyone knows us, because we are one of the island's few mixed Filipino families.

Swimming parallel with me, my island cousin's wife looked over at me through the sun's beaming rays and said, "You know ma'an, deres nuttin' West Indian about ya, 'cept ya Muddah."

I never claimed to understand all of my mother's culture. I had no clue how to be a "good West Indian daughtah."

"Give me an example of something a good West Indian daughter would do," I asked my cousin.

"Well, sah. If ya Muddah was sick, you would stop everything and go give her food, or you would make her food. Stoppin' for ya Muddah and run over to take care of her would be a good island daughtah 'ting to do, it shows how much you love her."

"Well, sah," I said to myself. "So to show Momma that I love her, I should cook for her when she's sick?" Revelation.

After that, as often as I could, I visited my mother like an island daughter would. I did everything I could to let her know how much I loved her, but our time together was almost over, and I knew I could never regain the time we'd already lost.

In the early winter of 2000, Phillip, my husband, drove us to Washington D.C. for what would be our final visit to Momma. Within six months, she would be dead, and our lifetime of issues would be buried. I rang the bell, turned the key, and opened the door to find Momma comfortably lounging across the living room sofa. With all of her nesting activities around her, she was watching television and was surrounded by her books, crossword puzzles, gadgets, knitting, snacks, and a tall glass of ice water. Once downstairs for the day, she remained on the first floor until evening. It was too painful for her to climb the stairs throughout the course of the day. She was perched on the living room sofa until bedtime.

"Hey, ma'an," I entered the living room and bent over to give her a welcoming kiss. I tried to embrace her, as it was the daughterly thing to do, and it was so hard for us to show affection toward each other. It had been a long time since she'd held me; in fact, I couldn't remember her ever holding me.

I took a seat across the room. My son, a toddler at the time, would run up to her, and then run back and forth, teasing her as toddlers do. Unable to get up from the sofa, she opened her arms wide to welcome him for a hug. He ran back to me, and jumped in my lap.

"He dun wan me edder..." Momma said with a somber hollowness in her eyes. Right there, I missed my chance to grab her for dear life and tell her how much I loved her.

"Momma, that's not true, he's just a toddler. Momma, let me cook you dinner. What would you like?"

"Where is Phillip, ma'an?"

"He's outside speaking with John and the neighbors, Momma. He'll be inside soon to see you...just relax. I'll roast some 'fallin' off the bone' baked chicken, some steamed buttered broccoli, and some macaroni and cheese for you. You sit back and enjoy your grandson."

"Rinse everything before you cook, ya hear me, ma'an." Momma was a stickler for sanitizing everything before cooking. That was the nurse in her.

Tell me ma'an, yah tell me. I wasn't the best island daughter I could have been. I didn't know how to be an island daughter, and she didn't know how to be a stateside mother. Momma enjoyed recipes from my mother-in-law's kitchen. I fumbled through her favorite recipe for cheese Bisquick biscuits, and Momma said I was a lousy baker because I never followed the recipe. Cooking for Momma was the only thing I could still do to try to be a "good West Indian daughtah." Maybe it would let her know how much I loved her, although it was probably too little, too late.

We had great expectations of each other which could never be satisfied.

Momma, my Asian Island mother. "Your mother looks like a Movie Star," the kudos of a lifetime. Momma was simply gorgeous and exotic, just beautiful.

THE WAR ZONE

My family's story begins with a simple love story. My parents met, fell in love, and had two children; my brother and me. It is a typical romance story of two beautiful people who met during their college years at Howard University in Washington, D.C., and wanted to make a life together during a tumultuous time in America. There is never a right time to fall in love, and it happens, even if it's risky business.

The years after World War II and the pre-season of the Civil Rights Movement was the era of their love affair. They met in the academic school year of 1946-47 and got married in 1949. They were a mixed race couple during a time when marrying across the racial divide in regions of America was illegal. I am not sure they considered how to have children in the midst of their decision. I was conceived in the middle of two internal American conflicts: the Cold War and America's War on Race. I was born in 1952 at D.C.'s Freedmen's Hospital. Poppa wheeled Momma to the nursery while he admired his first child and daughter.

I can imagine the day I was born. "Norma, she's beautiful. I suppose you were right. Your puppy, Sabina, will be jealous," Poppa exclaimed upon seeing his firstborn.

"Mrs. Holmes, we have to fill out the birth certificate. Have you named the baby," the doctor asked.

"Yes, Cheryl Denise. Cheryl is French for *beloved*, darling. I have always loved that name," my mother replied. "Horace, that will be it, O.K.?"

When Momma was very serious, she spoke with no accent at all. Horace nodded with delight.

"Mr. Holmes, fill out this information. Can I have your race, please?" the head nurse asked.

"Negro," Horace replied.

"Mrs. Holmes, and your race, please?" the head nurse asked my mother.

Inquisitive minds have always wanted to know Momma's race.

"Mrs. Holmes, we have to put something down. Please."

"Norma, look. We don't have much choice here. We can't keep it blank," my father said. There were no racial categorical boxes for my mixed race family to select other than "black." Back in my childhood, my father collapsed us all down into one box, keeping in-line with America's 1950s thinking. His plan was for us to just be an ambitious, hard-working Negro D.C. family.

"We are just going to be black folk and that's that," my father said.

However, taking all census racial and ethnic boxes into consideration, I am African-American and Philippine-American racially, and culturally, American, African American, Philippine-American, and West Indian.

Horace Holmes was a ray of hope for his family and ours. He was embraced early in his life by a junior high school teacher who took a special interest in him. She recognized his gifts and encouraged him to make something of himself. His dreams set himself apart from the other children, and his entire family recognized his success would be inevitable.

He was proud of having graduated from the exclusive Negro public prep high school, Dunbar High School in 1944. Originally The "M" Street School, Dunbar High was renamed after the poet Paul Laurence Dunbar, and it was originally regarded as *The Preparatory High School for Colored Youth.* One of my father's classmates told me about Dunbar in the 1940s.

"Cheryl, it was the place to be for Negro high school students, and admission was granted by a comprehensive interview process. You had to be light skinned, 'pedigreed mulatto.' Your skin had to be no darker than a brown paper bag, or if brown skinned, you had to be from a prominent family or show extreme promise," the source said. A pedigreed mulatto meant you could identify the source of your white blood, e.g. Sally Hemings' and Thomas Jefferson's cross-mixed DNA scenario.

"We all loved your father. I remember your mother being beautiful, but punitive socially for you, I am sure. Pretty, but not one of us, you know."

This is the way it was when my father's classmate and my father graduated in 1944. Horace went to college for a few months before enlisting in the Army in March, 1945. He served the remainder of World War II and an extra six months in Manila. He must have gotten a taste for those gorgeous Filipina women while he was there. Horace had passed the Civil Service typing exam as a young teen, so his keyboard skills kept him working in the Army Affairs office rather than the frontline.

In 1947, Horace returned from the war to finish both undergraduate and graduate degrees in Social Work from Howard University. He didn't expect to meet a young, mixed Filipina nurse from St. Thomas, the U.S. Virgin Islands. The little hands and feet of Norma Sabino, a petite woman with a five-foot body frame, told the true story of her Filipino ancestry. Her straight, black hair was always styled in island-twisted rolls and knots, and her hairstyles were always adorned with either a pink or white Virgin Island Hibiscus flower. Norma was often frustrated with her formless Asian hair and would whack it off, without fear, into a little short bob with chiseled bangs. Still, Norma's hair was beautiful, no matter the style.

Norma's skin-tone was like a mixed blend of smooth Irish Cream liqueur swirling over clear-ice rocks and floating in splendid Danish crystal stemware. Norma had short Asian forearms and sculpted legs. She had those deep Filipina dimples when she smiled, and her Filipina gene dominated her beauty with little trace of her maternal admixture of black and Irish. Putting it all together, Norma Sabino was some kind of pretty lady.

Norma wanted to be a registered nurse, and came to the United States to study nursing and medicine in 1946 at the Freedmen's Hospital School of Nursing. Upon entering the US immigration ports of Puerto Rico, she was classified as "white." Depending on her feelings about black folks from season to season, she would go in and out about being black. Due to anti-miscegenation laws in and outside of Washington at the time, she couldn't marry a white man as a mixed Filipina woman, and she couldn't be white and marry a black man. Also, she felt it would be disloyal to her Danish West-Indian culture to be anything else but black. Norma had made her choice, and wouldn't tell her exogamic multiracial children that they had a choice. Momma wasn't an African American woman, but a Philippine American woman. The gentlemen just loved her, especially Horace Holmes.

With a racial heritage of being white, black, and Amerindian, Horace was a good-looking, multi-racial D.C. native son in every sense of the term. He was a tall, lean, crisp, wavy-headed mulatto with marble green eyes. He could often be seen wearing a shark skin suit, a wool hat, a cashmere coat, and polished alligator shoes. Poppa was a Greek Alpha Phi Alpha letter fraternity brother. Even in college, Horace was focused on becoming the Mayor of D.C. someday. From the moment he completed his graduate degree in Social Work from

Howard University in 1951, to starting his career in the District's Juvenile Court system, Poppa played a unique, strategic role in D.C. politics.

The Echo Generation would refer to Momma and Poppa as MGMs, Multi-Generational Multi-racials. As Momma and Poppa met on their 1946-47 campus setting, the "sistahs" sense of entitlement to Horace threatened Norma. Norma had simply flipped her hair back and forth and snatched one of the most eligible men in D.C.; the "sistahs" were somewhat unforgiving for that. The only person who could've loved Horace Holmes more than Norma Sabino was Sadie, my paternal grandmother. Horace's choice for a wife caused a great deal of friction within his family network, and the reasons for that wouldn't become known to me until I was well into my adult years.

Sadie Lue-Sadie, Sadie, or Sadie Acty Holmes was stern-faced and had a displeasing countenance. She was married to my grandfather Landon Holmes, Sr., whom we called "Pops." One of our family mysteries was centered on Pops; we never knew if Pops was a white man or not. He sure looked like a white man to me. He kept us guessing, though no one dared to discuss his race. In fact, he was really keeping one big secret from us all.

Sadie and Pops migrated up from the farm working counties of Fauquier and Madison Counties Virginia to Washington, D.C. to make a life after the Great Depression. They were part of The First Great Negro Migration. They married each other's respective siblings, and nested with assorted other family members in the Foggy Bottom-

Georgetown district of Washington, District of Columbia. Georgetown, now gentrified, is D.C.'s trendy area near the trail of monuments, Watergate Towers, and the Potomac River waterways to Virginia.

Believe it or not, Georgetown was where the Negroes used to live.

They had four mulatto children, three sons and a daughter. Sadie gave birth to Landon, Jr., Thelma, Horace and Stanley. All of Sadie's sons were handsome mulatto men. They all married light-skinned mulatto Negro women. I think Aunt Bertha, Uncle Stanley's first wife, was a light-skinned Negro Amerindian mulatto woman. Aunt Mary was married to Uncle Landon and sure looked like a white woman.

My Poppa had a drop of Granny Sadie's indigo, and I think she favored him so much because she could see herself in him. All of the children had Pops' keen white features, eyes and "good Negro hair." Poppa's paternal family was your most Southern mulatto, that is to say they were "white lookin' folks." Sadie loved all of her children, but Poppa was very dear to her.

Sadie was relieved when her baby Horace returned from World War II. Horace wanted to go back to school, but couldn't afford it on the G.I. Bill alone. Sadie had saved the money Horace sent back home while he was in the service, knowing that her son would want to return to Howard. When he did return to school, she gave him enough money to last him the first quarter, and when that was gone, she opened another sacred bag of savings and handed him the money. Horace's education was worth the investment. That was the only honorable thing I have known her to do.

The year of my birth in 1952 was also the year that the Diary of Anne Frank was published in English, and it was a book I couldn't stop reading in elementary school. As the world read her story, I too was born into war. Night time raids and car bombs would occur right in the center of my home. My paternal family seemed as domestic terrorists to my parent's marriage, and the stereotypical deep brown skinned church lady, carrying a little black book with red letters, wearing a little black beanie hat, and long over-the-calf dresses which covered dark black stockings seemed to be the chief general of the opposing army. My paternal grandmother's main mission in life was to mortify her daughters-in-law, and it was Momma she focused her fury on.

I am confident that Momma's exotic beauty was the source of her problems with Sadie.

I remember my mother's nighttime, teary phone calls with Aunt Mary, rehashing Sadie's attacks, and I would find a quiet spot during those volatile moments when Sadie's bombings would occur in our home. I didn't understand Sadie's real concerns. If color was important, Sadie had a "white looking" man and good-looking mulatto children. Sadie was attractive, but in all honesty, her inner being was so haggard that it was hard to see her beauty. I could only see that she was spiteful, vindictive, and divisive when it came to my family.

As the firstborn, Poppa doted on me. He began keeping a folder of important documents on my life, and Momma kept a scrapbook of baby photos. The scrapbook, as well as anything else Momma cared about was organized in her single, personal file cabinet—*The Green Box.*

I remember the evening that Poppa brought it home.

The Green Box was an old Federal Government aluminum standing green file cabinet, and uniquely it was also a collapsible typing table. The desk portion folded down on one side and could easily flip-up to create a desktop. The cabinet top, when folded down, easily latched into the silver-square frame and its lock, to which Momma had the key. When opened, The Green Box had space enough for both legal and letter-sized green folders. My parents used it as a filing receptacle for vital and personal records, ancient and painful stories, photo negatives, and family secrets. Decades after they brought it home, The Green Box would save me.

Poppa and I bonded from the beginning, and at the same time my relationship with Momma began to unravel. When I was three years of age, Momma and I had one tough afternoon together. We were returning from her girlfriend's house at the very top of our street, and Momma must have said something not to my toddler liking. I remember spitting at her in retaliation. Momma swung around and slapped me.

Poppa came home from work to find me sitting on the floor at the front door with my bags packed.

"Hi baby," he said, trying to get through the door, but I was squatting at the threshold. "What's wrong, pun'kin?"

"Momma doesn't love me, Poppa. I want to leave. I want to go to a new home, Poppa. I just want to go," I explained.

"Norma? What's going on?" Poppa jumped his way over my fort at the front door entrance.

"Cher'rell says she wan' to leave, and I said go. Where's she gonna go? If Cher'rell has got somewhere else to go, she can go," Momma said. "Horace, you're spoilin' the child."

In Poppa's viewpoint, it didn't matter what happened that afternoon. He began to realize I was suffering with whatever Momma was going through. Who knew what was eating at her: being in America, not having her family, having Sadie as a mother-in-law? He came to my rescue over and over and over again. For some reason, Poppa took an upper hand in raising me, snatching me from my mother's ability to truly bond with me.

"You will never be like my mother, you will never be like my sister, and you will never be like your mother," he said to me often, allowing his words to take on the form of a mantra. I understood his desire for me not to be as his mother and sister, i.e., domestic workers. I never understood his reference to my mother, though. The only thing I understood was that she struggled to fit in a Negro

America as a racial and cultural oddity which forced him to intervene as he didn't want me to face the same challenges.

Determined to never return to his humble beginnings, he always had a plan for me. Regardless of my ignorance of Momma's race and cultural origins, I would be a well-bred, educated, astute, beautiful black woman.

"Cheryl, you're not going to be a maid like my mother and sister. You won't be poor like I was. Cheryl, you aren't going to be like your mother."

I was brainwashed, indoctrinated, empowered, or whatever you want to call it, into not thinking much about my mother's race or culture. I was left with not knowing her very well and not wanting to know her at all. Poppa raised me a womanist, and this frustrated Momma, as she seemed to have been taken out of the loop of my nurturing. We were almost literally ships passing across different sides of the Atlantic. Momma's solution?

"Horace, I want another baby and you can't have this one."

In the fall of 1956, Momma became pregnant again. They called a family meeting to tell me all about it. Momma had taught me to pray and sing "Jesus Loves Me," and every night I prayed until I fell asleep.

"Lord, I want a baby brother. Please Lord, I want a baby brother." I knew the Lord was watching me, as he always does, and sometimes, you get exactly what you pray for.

The baby was "soon come." I would put my ear to Momma's tummy, and each day, I could hear my baby brother moving. Momma was already considering how she would juggle two children in her hands. She asked Barbara, our back-door neighbor, to have her daughter Deborah walk me home from kindergarten. My time alone with Momma was already closing out.

Even my quiet time with Poppa would soon be compromised, as everything was focused around the arrival of a new family member. At the beginning of Momma's career, she worked the night shift at Freedmen's Hospital and she'd succeeded in her goal of becoming a registered nurse. Momma's night shift gave me wonderful time with Poppa, though given Momma's pregnancy, he was sure to pick her up in the evenings.

"Cheryl, let's go. We have to be on time to get Momma, and I want to take a walk along 14th street. I want to buy Dinah Washington's new 78 R.P.M vinyl album," Poppa said. It was at a record store on 14th St. that Poppa bought my first R.P.M. record, Elvis Presley's "Hound Dog."

"Poppa, can I have a piece of bubble gum too? I am saving the wrappers for a prize," I said, and he'd always make sure I got a piece of bubble gum.

"Sure, baby anything you want," was often his reply, often to Momma's angst.

I would glare at the men wearing little red bow ties when we walked down the street. They were holding newspapers, shouting something about a man named Elijah Muhammad. He was frightening to me when he appeared on the cover of their newspaper. His strange-looking hat with stars all around it was the most startling. The diagonal moon appeared as an eye stalking me.

The street was always crowded with the hustle and bustle of shops and the making of business. Like 125th Street in Harlem, 14th Street Northwest, Washington was the place for Negroes for gathering and "limin" (the island term for having fun or relaxing). Commerce disappeared during the riots after Dr. Martin Luther King Jr. was assassinated. I smile when I visit the street now and see the white tourists, shoppers and college crowds up and down 14th street. White folks would have never dared to walk 14th street, "black in the day." It's not that they wouldn't have been accepted, there was just a lot of black culture to digest.

After our walk, Poppa and I would drive over to the Howard U. campus to pick up Momma from work. The hospital was at the bottom of the campus corridor. The Wonder Bread Bakery was directly across the street from the hospital, blanketing the neighborhood in the fragrance of warm bread.

We would approach the hospital's circle driveway and wait for Momma to come out to Poppa's latest fancy car around 11 p.m., and did Poppa ever love his fancy cars. The car door would swing open from within and Momma would get in the car with a smile. Momma was so beautiful in her uniform. She wore her nursing pin and class ring with pride. Poppa would give her a welcoming kiss, and I would squirm in the back seat until it was over. Peace like that was a blessing between family battles in the war with Sadie, and there was always a battle coming.

I have been regarded as colored, Negro, black, Afro-American, African- American. So please don't mind my interchanging terms for being "black in the day."

My parents met in college. After graduation, they were married. The anti-miscegenation laws prevented my mother from marrying a white man as a mixed Filipina and prevented her from marrying a black man as a white woman. Momma became "colored" in order to marry an African-American.

1957

Born in 1957, Chico (Granny Sabino gave Horace Holmes, Jr. his nickname the moment she received our phone call that he had arrived) looked just like Momma. He had her olive coloring and very straight, black, Asian hair. I didn't think I looked like either of my parents. I began to wonder if I was adopted and that they hadn't told me the truth. Chico's likeness to Momma actually began to drive a wedge between Momma and me, worsening the divide that was already there.

"Well, Chico and I can go to Glen Echo, you and Poppa can't go," Momma would tease. Glen Echo Park was one of Metro D.C.'s best amusement parks, though blacks weren't allowed in. Momma was right in that she and baby Chico could pass for white and get into the park, yet me and Poppa couldn't. Despite my white skin, my curly hair would've been a giveaway.

To this day, I don't know which parent I look like.

I think Poppa and his circle of associates could be likened to the cast of characters featured in E. Franklin Frazier's 1957 book, *The Black Bourgeoisie.* Frazier coined the phrase "social amnesia" to describe the chronic social condition whereby Negroes who find success don't look back to their meager beginnings, and strive to become a part of the black bourgeoisie. As Poppa's work was beginning to pay off, I think that Poppa had to struggle with our mixed-race family issues, maybe more than Momma.

In the early days of the family war, Poppa's family always seemed to arrive at our home in tribal formation. They needed each other in order to process reconnaissance. They would arrive as a caravan, usually on Sundays after their Holiness church service. Out of all the cars, it was the steam rolling, dark colored Nash that I had to watch out for. The Nash was American Motors' popular sedan; a mix between a rocket and an armored car. It was General Sadie's tank. I can't even remember how many would arrive, but this I know for sure, my little immediate family was surrounded and outnumbered. Momma trusted not a one of them, so she never let me out of her sight. Baby Chico, asleep in his crib, would be spared the horrors of war...for now.

The first thing these creatures of habit would do is leer at me. Pops and Uncle Landon would gawk at me like I was a young calf headed to the Montgomery County 4H state fair. After that, Uncle Landon would look at Momma, and then look at me again. Back, and forth, back, and forth. The poor man couldn't make sense of the picture.

Sadie slipped from one corner of the living room to the other planning strategy against Momma. Aunt Mary was Momma's only line of defense, whispering jokes in her ear about Sadie. Momma would have one eye on me, and one ear listening to Aunt Mary. Momma had to stay sharp; the rules of engagement changed every visit.

Poppa would attempt to ease the tension by serving a little "fire water," which is a mix between ginger ale and bourbon. He served his "High Ball" recipe in a tall, frosty chilled glass, and topped it off with cherries floating on top of fresh crystal ice cubes. Poppa made sure to toss a few of the red jewels my way. It was the family's favorite drink. Then again, the closest Sadie and Pops came to drinking was the wine at Holy Communion. Besides, Sadie needed to stay focused. They were sanctified folks, of course; we were religious Episcopalians.

Uncle Landon, good and relaxed now, with his head still swiveling from side-to-side, would just start a smackin' his lips and the High Ball would do the rest of the talking for him.

"Norma, you look like you put on a little weight," Uncle Landon said.

I was thinking to myself, "Uncle Landon, Momma just had a baby," and at the time, Momma had been on a diet for days. I was worried about Momma, even though I knew that they were coming for me next. Thank God for Aunt Georgetta and Aunt Julia, Pops' sisters. They ran interference and granted me a few minutes grace.

"Hello, shuggie, I'm your Aunt Georgetta from Pittsburgh. You're just pretty as a picture, pretty as a picture," Aunt Georgetta would nod toward Aunt Julia in agreement. They'd smile together and agree, "That's right, just pretty as a picture, pretty as a picture." Aunt Georgetta would grab her daughter's hand and say "Marlene, isn't she just pretty as a picture?"

Aunt Georgetta, Aunt Julia, and Cousin Marlene, Poppa's first paternal cousin, were such a white-looking family, and they were all from Pittsburgh. However, Cousin Marlene, in addition to always having the right of way with Momma, also possessed the secret of our family's makeup, which she would only reveal to me after many years.

Uncle Landon and Pops came back in after looking at the new 1957 White T-Bird, and my belly churned. Poppa was standing close as he always did, but not even he could save me all of the time.

"Lil' Cheryl, you sure are fat, aren't you baby," Uncle Landon would say, standing side-by-side with Pops like *Amos n' Andy*.

Momma would get excited and speak in words only God could understand. "Ma'an only a dog dus like a bone; 'dah chil' is healtee," Momma said, or rather, I think she said. Somehow, the drama would always turn back on Momma. It would always appear that Momma was the culprit, not Sadie.

Sadie never said a word to me.

Sadie launched her scud missiles, and I always got caught in the fallout. It was the same scenario every family visit. Afterward, Momma and Poppa would argue through the early evening, and the arguments would end with Poppa leaving and saying he was going to his mother's house. The drama between visits carved a hole in Momma's heart as well.

Momma was left crying and empty-hearted. The situation put Poppa in the impossible place to make a choice between his mother and his wife. From Momma's perspective, leaving the house after arguments would be a non-verbal decision in favor of Sadie. If he had a third option, I think he would've headed over to Uncle Landon's for a High Ball. I would whimper into the evening until he was safe at home again, afraid that he wouldn't return.

In between warfare episodes, we had a great time within our family unit and Poppa's siblings. We rode in Poppa's fancy cars, dined at the Hot Shoppes (now the Marriott Hotel) for a special treat, took late night excursions to watch the airplanes land over the Potomac River, got lemon frozen custard at the Rhode Island Avenue frozen custard shop, and checked out the cars at Thacker Motors, a used Cadillac dealer in the area. Poppa loved his Caddies. Poppa captured Super 8 mm movies of great family trips and outings. We had warm moments together without the Sadie situation taunting our lives.

On Friday nights, we visited Uncle Landon and Aunt Mary, driving past the new hamburger franchise on South Dakota Avenue. We stopped at the burger joint with the golden arches where for 47 cents we got a three course meal and ate the best fries in town. Uncle Landon and Aunt Mary were marvelous away from Sadie's army. An evening together promised conversation about cars, family gossip, and lots of laughing over Aunt Mary's Sadie jokes. Aunt Mary would curl her nose up and say "Oh, Mary don't be face-shush," imitating Sadie's attempts at using verbose vocabulary and butchering the word 'facetious'.

No matter how Mary felt about Sadie or Poppa's family, she attended all the funerals, kept all of the obituaries, and kept track of the entire crew and their news updates. In truth, I think she loved her in-laws, but stood with Momma for the sake of being a good sister-in-law. Aunt Mary loved Momma, too. High Balls made Aunt Mary funnier and funnier, and I loved her Jackie Gleason impressions. Her favorite saying overall was *"Amen Brother Ben, shot the turkey, killed the hen..."*

Now in her elderly years, Aunt Mary was diagnosed with a little dementia, and she doesn't need the family libation to fuel her sense of humor anymore. Her caretaker admits that she keeps the elder care party going with her abominable, off-color jokes that you can't help but laugh at. She can still remember every joke she ever told during our Friday visits, even if she can't remember the visits themselves.

"Aunt Mary, don't worry, I have everything covered," I say when I assure Aunt Mary of her present affairs. Her reply is always the same.

"Like the rug said to the bug, 'I got ya covered," she exclaims. Her raspy laugh comforts me that she is well.

"How's your Momma?" Aunt Mary asks.

"Momma's gone now, Aunt Mary, remember?"

"Oh, yeah, and what about Sadie?"

"Gone longer than Momma."

"Oh yeah, the good die young and old devils never die, they just fade away. One never knows, do one," Mary says, concluding her routine.

Momma and Poppa had great friends and they all seemed to love us so much more than our own family. Friday night entertainment would always precede Saturday night visits to friends at my parent's former apartment building on 19th Street in Northwest D.C. They accepted Momma like Poppa's people couldn't and were a colorful, memorable presence in Momma and Poppa's lives. Uncle Jack was another debonair, clean-cut mulatto gent who looked like he was Lebanese and had a slapstick-comedy persona. Famous for his jokes, humor was his gift to our family. He was the very best of friends with my father even unto death. Aunt Virginia was tall, slender, lean, and had a fashion model's elegance. I suppose being a striking couple didn't make for a perfect marriage, because they divorced as I got older. Uncle Jack would stay close to our lives; Aunt Virginia would vanish away to be replaced by Aunt June.

June was a sharp, tiny, pristine, and beautiful woman with a little cropped snatch-back hairstyle. She stole the hearts of everyone in our immediate family and was a blessed stabilizer for Uncle Jack. Aunt June was patient, always listening to my emotional cries for Momma. June's wisdom prevailed, and she resolved to never get between Momma and me. She didn't know enough about the issues between us to act as the solution.

We visited Uncle Wes and Aunt Mamie on the weekends, too. Aunt Mamie got "saved" and "healed" while praying to a black velvet background painting of Jesus in their hallway. She had a tumor which disappeared, and the miracle converted her. Wes and Mamie got divorced along the way. Aunt Mamie truly made an acute turn toward Jesus and the church. I thought she was part Chinese. Slender, very fair skinned with slanted Asian eyes, Aunt Mamie was definitely a mulatto woman, but she had to have been mixed with something more. Her house was full of black lacquer, high polished Chinese furnishings and appointments. It all suggested she was Asian somewhere in the story of her background. The black velvet ceiling-to-floor painting of Jesus greeted you the moment she opened the door; I always will remember it as the miracle painting. After she'd converted, she retired from the party life that my parents were enjoying. She stopped the casual smoking, stripped her hair of all straightening treatments, and actually proclaimed that the Lord had given her a recipe for a natural straightening cream. She began using her Johnson and Johnson-like concoction stuff in her hair, but I couldn't tell if it made a difference. The God-given potion took its place in her lineup of miracles, all attributed to praying to the miracle painting. She stopped drinking and dancing. When she and Wes divorced, she started "A House of Prayer" ministry, thus becoming Momma's most important Christian advisor and prayer partner.

I always hoped that the Sadie issue would disappear, but it never did. Things would quiet down for a season and give way to great times, and in those great times, Momma was making her own plans—keeping herself and the children away from Poppa's crazy family. Unfortunately, Poppa learned of these plans rather early on.

"Hey baby," Poppa said to me, coming home from work on a winter 1957 evening. "Norma, I'm home."

"Hey, ma'an. Dinner will be ready in a few," Momma said as Poppa entered the kitchen. The kitchen was in its usual immaculate state, and Momma was cutting green peppers on a cutting board. It was the typical homecoming in the Holmes residence, complete with the wonderful scent of pepper sauce wafting through the house and Momma's Calypso music entertaining her while she cooked.

"What are we having?"

"I'm shelling shrimp. Gonna sauté them with onions and green peppers. Making cod fish cakes too."

"Alright. We'll talk after dinner," Poppa said. After dinner, Poppa took his usual seat in front of the T.V. to smoke a cigarette and watch the news. Momma entered the living room, wiping her hands on her torn apron before removing it. She hung it on a rack near the kitchen threshold.

"What did you want to talk about," Momma probably asked my father.

"My mother spoke with my father today, and he told me something disturbing," I can imagine Poppa replied.

"O.K.?"

"He said that you don't want my mother to watch the kids anymore because she doesn't speak well, and you don't want the kids to be influenced by poor English."

"Where did she get that idea from?"

"Mary told her. Mary said that you told her last night over the phone. Norma, did you say that to Mary?"

"Well, it's true, isn't it?"

"So you did say that to Mary?"

"I don't care who said what. It's true, isn't it?"

"Norma, it may be true, but we need the help. You need the help."

"Your mother is always making melee. This is why I don't want her around."

"So you said it?"

"I'm not saying I did or didn't. I'm saying your mother is always making trouble. Why would she listen to Mary and then tell Pops? Look at this mess she started."

Poppa picked up his ashtray, and crushed his cigarette into it. He stood up and said "Enough, Norma. I'm going to go visit my family."

"You're going to leave? I want you to stay with us tonight."

"I'm going out."

"For how long?"

"I don't know."

"Horace, you leave me here with these children tonight, you might as well not come back."

"Norma, don't threaten me. I'm going to my mother's and that's that."

"You leave and just don't come back, you hear me, ma'an?"

"Don't challenge me. I'll go to my mother's house when I please."

Poppa headed out of the door, and Momma flew upstairs, crying. I would ask Momma if Poppa was coming back soon, and she couldn't answer. Sadie arguments always embittered our dinner.

The pressure of my baby brother's arrival was added to the list of things I would worry about as I entered kindergarten in 1957, right up there with polio. The Look and Life magazine pictures of children with polio wearing braces may have been frightening, though not as frightening as the idea of getting a polio shot from Dr. Cardozo. He gave me my physical exam and all the shots, you know, the ones that would make your arm stiff in the morning.

Kindergarten became a volatile, uncertain space all by itself.

"The Russians are coming. The Russians are coming. Get ready and build your bomb shelter. This is a test of the Emergency Broadcast System," I would hear daily. I was starting to learn the true meaning of John Cameron Swayze's Timex watch commercial, "It Takes A Licking And Keeps On Ticking," which ended the newscast each night. Russia's Khruschev and Cuba's Castro were always the villains against America's Eisenhower and Kennedy; the brand-new peacock color vision programming came on in the evening to tell the stories.

I was so disappointed when the Chet Huntley-in New York, David Brinkley-Washington, D.C. "Good Nites" replaced Swayze's

1956 newscast. Eventually, Poppa would favor Walter Cronkite coming into our home nightly and scaring me to death. Then, the neighborhood sirens test would blast the Civil Defense alarms. At any given hour during the school day, we would have bomb drills. We would line up single file and walk quietly along the Hallway's edge. "Sit Indian style with your heads in your laps until the bell rings again," Mrs. Carroll said referring to the glorious 12 o'clock bell.

Momma would meet me in our class' coat room at noon and help me cloak up for going outdoors. In the winter, we struggled to get my little thick thighs into my red leggings. We would start our walk home together stopping at the local District Grocery Store. I loved those little cartons of waxed cola bottles filled with colored sugar water. I would sort them in my head first and then graduate them in order-by-color sequence. I also liked those Mary Jane maple candies, but the wax cola bottles were my favorite choice. Momma would buy them for me. One at a time, I would snap off the wax top with my teeth, suck the juice out and chew the entire wax bottle like chewing gum. The colors were pretty, and so was Momma. I can't say it enough; Momma was beautiful. I wished that I looked like her, but I didn't look like her at all.

Momma had funny little ways that we would just call "islandy." For example, she believed that if we didn't sweep the floor before sunset, we would have misfortune.

"Ma'an, hurry up and sweep da kitchen before we dus get bad luck, hurry up and sweep before da sun goes down," she would say during after-dinner chores. Recently, I had to catch myself and chuckle as my daughter was performing her gymnastic split routine on my kitchen floor, and my son stepped over her sprawled out legs. I could just hear Momma saying, "Step back over her meh'son, go back over hah da way you came." Islandy superstitions haunt me even now--you see, an islandy belief is that walking over someone would stunt the growth of one of their limbs. The only way to prevent it was to walk back over the person.

Momma loved soap operas, and she had ever since she lived on the islands where Spanish soap operas would broadcast from Puerto Rico beginning at six in the evening. Seeing my family gather around soaps for myself on my first visit to the islands, I never believed my mother's people understood a word of Spanish. Yet, they would watch and laugh as if they knew exactly what was happening. Momma was in high heaven watching the CBS soaps while tackling crossword puzzles. The soap opera pocket size magazines and crossword puzzle books were all full of recipe index cards that were being used as bookmarks. Momma loved to cook. She would clip recipes, write them down, and teach me how to cook her island recipes as well as her latest favorite recipes. I never followed the measurements.

Our bookshelves around the house were lined with island trinkets and tchotchkes. Momma had quite the collection of ash trays, demitasse cups, spoons, crystal pieces, island black face dolls, and assorted Virgin Island souvenirs. The house was a gallery of beautiful island art. Our bookshelves were lined up with cook books, Virgin Island Creole dictionaries, glossaries, and history books detailing the past of the U.S. Virgin Islands. Between those books, Momma's nursing scrapbook, and her wedding album, a wealth of family and island history was in our home. I couldn't understand most of it at the time, save Momma's nursing scrapbook and wedding album. Organized in the living room table drawer was a loose stack of pictures of the family she had left back in the islands and a folded paper outlining the family tree. Connecting the dots of her family's photographic history was difficult without understanding the timeline of WWI and the history of the Middle Passage, specifically the Ghanaian and Danish slave trade. Momma considered these pictures to be sacred. We would look at them often, but she never really explained much about them on her own.

Momma had lots of pictures of her mother, my Granny Sabino. My grandmother's name was Amelia Amanda Collins Sabino, and Momma looked nothing like her. Momma also had this picture of a deep brown, thin woman in a beautiful linen dress. This was Granny Sabino's mother, Bada, a dark brown woman who is my maternal great grandmother. In another stack of pictures were old tattered pictures of this funny little Asian, Chinese-Oriental looking Filipino man in a Navy uniform. Those pictures were the most precious of the bunch. There were two very old photographs of a white man with a handle bar moustache and a photographic studio career portrait of another white captain-like sailor with a walking stick and an anchor at his feet. These were pictures of Momma's Filipino father, her mother's paternal Irish father-her grandfather, and her Irish great grandfather, Charles Collins. These were all pictures of Momma's "people dem"--they were all Momma's family, not *mine*.

Momma's family photos told the tale of Sinforoso Jose Sabino, my maternal Filipino grandfather. He was deployed on the Navy yacht, the U.S.S. Vixen, which was headed to the Danish West Indies after the sale of the Virgin Islands to the U.S. from Denmark in 1917. In 1913, Woodrow Wilson segregated the armed services. Colored Navy mess laborers were replaced by U.S. colonized Filipino mariner men trained to be servant replacements. Sinforoso from Cavite, Philippines woke up one morning in the Danish West Indies on Transfer Day March 31, 1917, finding himself on the golden sands of paradise.

Granny Sabino, along with many young island women, volunteered at the USO. She met Sinforoso when the U.S. Navy hit the shores of paradise. They got married in 1918, and The Reformed Church of St Thomas, in their 1920 newsletter, *The Christian Intelligencer* recorded the wedding:

"Rev. and Mrs. Folensbee, arrived at St. Thomas July 6, 1918, just a year and six months ago, and in that time they have had seven weddings. On July 29, 1918, Amelia Amanda Collins was married to Sinforoso Jose Sabino, a sailor on the U.S.S. Vixen and born in the Philippine Islands."

He gave my island Granny three Asian babies; the last baby was my mother. He disappeared three years later and was never seen again. That is the unfortunate reality of war abandonment. Momma brought his baggage with her to America.

In a tattered envelope, she had pictures of her male admirers. She never claimed any as boyfriends or companions. The inscriptions on the backs of the pictures confirmed them as admirers only. She didn't mind Poppa seeing them, because she only had eyes for him and he knew it. There were pictures of men from around the world and of all nationalities. There were so many different faces, and I couldn't even begin to tell their racial backgrounds. They all wanted Norma's attention. Momma's beauty had drawn them near.

Momma always figured I wasn't interested in the coffee table drawer contents, and I wasn't because it all looked pretty strange to me. I didn't mind looking at the pictures and hearing the stories, but I couldn't bond with the story of my funny looking Asian grandfather meeting my island grandmother as my own story. Momma's life picture stories were tucked in the living room's coffee table for 62 years and only came out on rainy days and cold, lonely nights. The folded paper site mapping the family would find me again in life.

From the island, Granny Sabino would send Momma an array of precious goods every week. Granny Sabino, who loved charms and charm bracelets as much as the next girl, would always have some special little island jewelry for me. Granny Sabino lived so far away, but was more "grand muddah" to me than Granny Sadie, who was minutes away. I can count the times on two hands that I had actually seen Granny Sabino because the distance and cost made seeing her prohibitive. On one special occasion of seeing her, she slipped her signature charm bracelet on my arm.

"Ma'an, it a' tal I have me'chil, ya me blood," Granny Sabino said when she gave me the bracelet.

Momma would place a Trans-Atlantic call to Granny Sabino every Sunday morning, and the overseas operator would return it in the evening. The phone was passed from foreign family member to foreign family member, each speaking to us one at a time. They were my family, but I would only actually see them a few times in my life. There was Blanchie, Momma's cousin and my god mother; Fifie, my great aunt and Granny's sister; and Uncle Cito, my mother's brother. Their Virgin Island Creole was fast tongued, and they would speak even faster to hurry the call and save money. They missed Momma, and I knew they loved me, somehow, from afar. Precious moments with Momma's family were the true ease I got from the madness of Poppa's family.

Chico was so cute when he would crawl on top of Momma's coffee table for playtime. He had no idea of the pictures in the drawer and the story they told. The Lord heard my prayer and gave the family the favored son. As a result, I began to slip into solitary activities. I would go outside on the lawn for hours looking for four-leaf clovers. I would hang out with the family next door, and their daughter Anita would paint my nails pearly-pink while we watched the dancing on American Bandstand together in the afternoons.

Months went by, and I gained the confidence to be alone more often. I walked the neighborhood, going from house to house as though I didn't have a home. I would circle the neighborhood. I never ate at the kitchen tables of so many neighbors. "Don't eat from strangers," Momma said, although the fact that she never called for me worried me. Maybe it was an island thing to just open the door and let the kids go out for an afternoon. I suppose she trusted the neighbors, which might be naïve thinking for 50's Washington, D.C. Still, she let me go on my own.

I concluded my neighborhood tours before 5 p.m. so that I could catch Poppa coming home from work. Momma didn't go back to work immediately after giving birth to Chico, so our time together for picking up Momma from the hospital was over. Meeting Poppa before dinner became my favorite time with him. Most of the time, Momma was wrapped up in caring for the new baby. All I had was Poppa.

"Hello, hello," Poppa would always say coming into the house with a tiny bubble gum machine toy for me. He'd kiss Momma, grab a seat in his favorite chair, reach for a cigarette, and cross his legs to relax.

Evenings with Poppa, with me in his arms, and the entire family watching NBC's "The Nat King Cole Show" were certain to include a few cigarettes and the occasional pipe.

I hear Sinatra's distinct wail when I think of 1957.

It was a very good year.

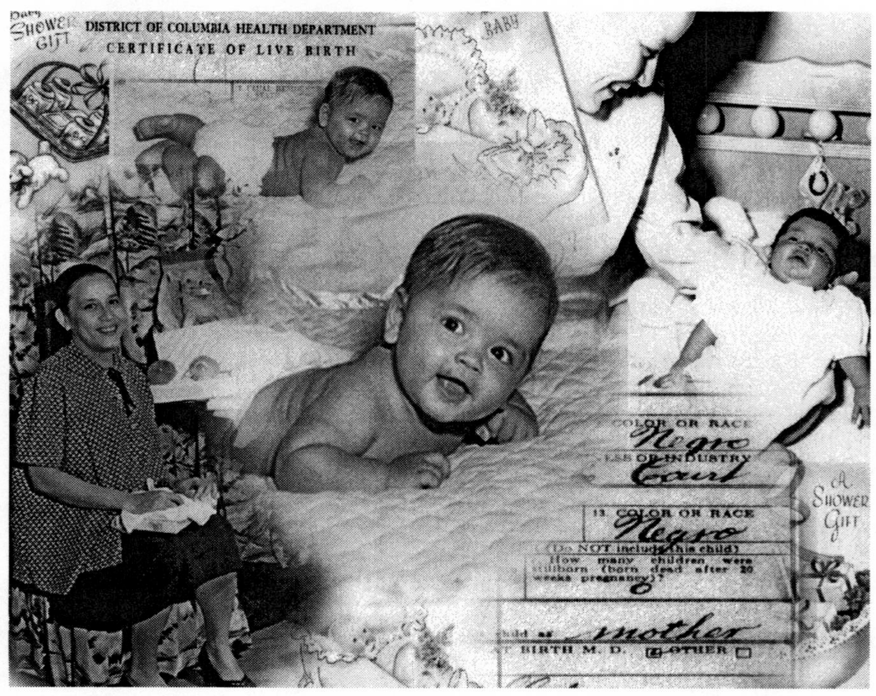

My mother regarded herself as "NEGRO" on my birth certificate. America's "One Drop" ruling regarded me as "NEGRO." There were no multiracial categories available to classify my baby boomer, Washington, D.C. birth.

UP AND ACROSS TOWN

Visiting Uncle Bob and Aunt Rita, my god parents, over on 19th Street was a treat in 1957 and beyond. Aunt Rita was a government employee by day, painter by night who produced the most wonderful works I'd ever seen. I would watch her work, and she gifted me with my first set of oil paints. I was mesmerized by her ability to capture reality on canvas, and I prayed that I would be able to do the same thing someday.

I came to the realization that I wanted to be an artist at such a young age because I was surrounded by so many inspirational, artistic people when I was younger. Ed Hubbard, one of the first black photographers in the area, photographed our family as if we were movies stars, especially Momma. Being the marvelous hosts that they were, Ed and his wife, Dot, served us Vienna sausages and cheese squares whenever we went to their fascinating apartment. They loved us so, but the only thing on Ed's mind when Momma came over was to take pictures of her. Momma must've loved the attention. She would run her fingers through her hair, look straight into Ed's camera lens, and Ed would snap pictures of the gorgeous Filipina woman until his film ran out.

I would watch his large hands as they were able to grasp two or three cameras at a time. Ed had a darkroom in his bathroom, and I would follow him into that red-lit room to catch a glimpse of the scientist at work. He seemed to carry all of his cameras and photographic gear around his neck all at the same time. Ed would slip out in the middle of our visits telling us that he needed to fix his old lemon Jaguar. This was a convenient excuse to engage in other evening activities.

Not only a proud Alpha Phi Alpha man, Poppa was also an active part of a men's social club, "The Viceroys." Mr. Mackie, one of Poppa's Viceroy friends, taught art at D.C.'s technical high schools. Attending Viceroy dances gave Poppa opportunities to promote that I was a budding artist. I sent Poppa to his dances with a folded drawing in his pocket hoping that Mr. Mackie would assess my ability.

"Poppa, what did Mr. Mackie say," I asked Poppa in the mornings after his black tie dinners. "Can I draw? Do I have talent, Poppa?"

Mr. Mackie offered to help me, but Poppa couldn't see me going to the tech school where he was the art teacher. Poppa didn't like the D.C. neighborhood where Mr. Mackie taught even if Poppa was intrigued by my interest in art. My coloring and drawing skills began to grow as solitary space became more and more familiar to me. I kept busy with art projects while watching "I Love Lucy," my favorite television show in the late 1950's.

"Momma, Momma, I Love Lucy is on. Come on, it's on," I cried out, while watching television upstairs one evening. Momma was downstairs, ironing in the kitchen, and baby Chico was cribbed in the living room. I ran to the top of the stairs with so much excitement that I tripped and fell down the flight of stairs.

"Momma."

She never came for me. I laid there until I could get up on my own. It took a moment, but I got up on my own. I walked into the kitchen.

"Momma, I fell down the steps. I Love Lucy is on. Why didn't you come for me when I called for you," I asked her, and I very much had wanted her to help me when I'd called for her.

"You got up, didn't you," Momma replied.

"Momma, you can have that baby, you and that baby I prayed for, you can have each other just fine," I snapped. Our emotional gap was created in that moment, and would never truly close.

A mass exodus of white and Jewish families moving west out of D.C.'s Rock Creek Park to the higher grounds of Maryland left only one "black in the day" D.C. neighborhood to aspire toward living in: the upper northwest blocks of 16th Street. Almost literally a "Canaan in D.C.," the 16th Street sign on both ends of its neighborhood corridor might as well have been road signs pointing out of D.C.'s Negro wilderness and into a spot for upward mobile Negroes in search of milk and honey.

In 1961, Mr. and Mrs. Holmes took a private tour of one of the homes on 16th Street.

"My husband and I built this home, you will notice all of the hand painting, done by an Italian painter," the home's owner told the young mixed-race couple. The proud homeowner showed the couple the home's powder room. "Notice the powder room painting. It is of a Parisian window view…it gives the powder room depth, don't you think?"

The homeowner turned to me. "Oh little one, wait until we get upstairs. There is a pink ballerina painted on my daughter's wall. You will just adore it." The homeowner refocused on Mr. and Mrs. Holmes. "The chandeliers are imported. Each piece is crystal, and we had the drapes custom-made just for the house. All of this will stay. Please don't paint over the walls…we've enjoyed them so much."

"Well, Mr. Holmes, what do you think? How about you Mrs. Holmes? I know the children just love it…don't you kids? The house asking price is $27,000 dollars; we'll get you a great mortgage."

"It sounds like a good deal," Mr. Holmes announced. "I will need the price in homeowners and mortgage insurance first. I need to look at all of the costs, like the electricity and gas bills."

In the school year of 1961-62, we moved on up.

I had finally settled into elementary school, and the truth was Poppa's new plan to move was a terrible disruption. It was far too much change to make at once, and there were way too many adjustments for us to make as a family. I really felt bad for Momma because she couldn't manage our upgrade in living. Her friends, her shopping, and her hobbies weren't within walking distance. Momma's experiences with driving weren't favorable. They were funny but not favorable.

During a visit from Sadie's clan, I saw Momma standing directly behind a little blue and white Studebaker that Poppa bought for her. Pops was in the front seat. The minute Pops stepped on the gas pedal to rev it up the car backfired, spewing a black fume and soot up and down Momma's leg. Completely flustered, Momma threw her hands to the air and ran toward the porch.

"Ma'an, I'm through."

"Norma, where are you going? Come back," Poppa pleaded. Momma never drove again in my childhood, and Poppa sold the car.

Back in our old neighborhood, Momma and I walked everywhere together, and she would even hold my hand. We would walk up to the Newton Street movie theatre for the latest Disney movies, and we would go roller skating on Saturdays at the St. Anthony's Catholic Church School's gym. I adored roller skating at their Saturday afternoon skating hour. When we were there, Momma usually bought me a Dr. Pepper. On the way to the gym was Woolworth's, and Momma was certain to stop there. As a brilliant seamstress, Momma liked to look at the material cloth and sewing patterns. She made many of my dresses with the materials she bought at Woolworth's.

Knowing Poppa as I did, his Northeast neighborhood selection for our first home had to have been strategic. He knew that we were a "passin' black" family, so I'm sure he thought about where we fit within the colored matrix of good D.C. neighborhoods. Poppa cared about the desires of his heart, not color barriers. However, the move unearthed and disoriented Momma socially to the point that she never recovered from it. My elementary school transfer became an issue during our relocation, as there was an interesting alternative to consider other than registering at the new neighborhoods' closest school. D.C. had launched its first magnet school experiment, The Margaret M. Amidon Program. Handpicked students across D.C. were carefully selected and invited to attend the pilot magnet school as student guinea pigs.

Amidon Elementary School was located in what is now the fashionable Southwest section of our nation's capital. The area, not so vogue then, was the location of several military barracks and the city's extremely low-income housing. The neighborhood was typical to any devastated urban, at risk community. What an odd place to test a magnet school curriculum. The program also extended its advanced curriculum to the junior high school next door, Jefferson Jr. High School. Washington's finest young scholars traveled from all points around the city to attend the program.

Poppa made sure I was in those numbers.

I didn't want to change schools. At my old school, I was learning French at the time and had been selected to study music. Somehow, I could easily understand French, and that was important for me. In music, I found a great sense of accomplishment since I wasn't excelling in physical education. I was finally being chosen for something in spite of my odd little self.

"Cheryl, I want you to take these sticks and tap as well as count when I point to the music notes," the music teacher taught me. Tightening my grip around the black drumsticks, I proceeded to follow her every word.

"Mrs. Holmes, Cheryl was tested for her musical skills a few days ago. Your daughter has the ability to embrace music lessons here at the school. We would like her to be in the school band," my music teacher told Momma after school several days later. My road to musical stardom ended with the move to Northwest 16th St. and my transfer to MMA. I was never fulfilled in the school environment again until I entered design college, although I was still happy with the way things were progressing. We had to move and advance along up the social and economic ladder, and I understand now that sacrifices had to be made. Our emotional well-being was offered upon the altar.

"Cheryl, my mother knows your mother," one of my new classmates came running to tell me as I entered into the new school during its mid-year. I was a little stunned, wondering how this girl even knew I was there. "My mommy wants your mother to call her, she has a job for your mother."

Momma was popular in the Howard University medical community. Everyone knew Momma on campus from her Freedmen's Hospital's nursing school days. Medicine was a neutral ground and a common denominator for her and having her Howard University friends. The doctors adored Momma as she was without selfishness and full of compassion when it came to their patients. Momma had that Florence Nightingale touch.

When infirmed, you want a Filipina nurse by your side.

Though I didn't know the messenger, I did give Momma the message, and there was indeed a job waiting just for her. Momma and my friend's mother had been classmates. My friend's mother was the head nurse on her job, and was looking for a registered nurse to fill a staff position. Momma started working at the student health service on the campus of Howard University. Momma enjoyed returning to her career, and it gave her a social outlet. It was good for Momma to return to work, and the outlet would prove to be valuable as the years progressed.

We began a new daily routine in a new neighborhood, a new elementary school and with Momma returning to work. Now, each day began with Poppa dropping baby brother off at St. Luke's Episcopal Church's nursery school followed by our dropping Momma off for work at Howard's campus. Poppa and I had at least a half hour of driving time together through rush hour traffic to Southwest D.C. Poppa and I grew closer together while Momma and I drifted apart. That's how it would be for the rest of my childhood regarding my mother.

By the time I completed elementary school, I think Momma and Poppa realized I was struggling socially and made plans for me to go to private school. They secured an interview for me to attend the National Cathedral School for Girls, but that's as far as my application went. Crossing over Wisconsin Avenue to the white side of town for school wasn't an easy consideration, either. My survival skills for succeeding in the D.C. public school system kept reinforcing my independence. My identity as a young D.C. black tween and teenager was being carved out. I was becoming just what Poppa felt was best for me—the best young black woman I could be in America.

"Cheryl, we grew up differently, you and me," my brother said to me when we were both past middle-age. While I was attending MMA, he attended the St. Alban's Cathedral School for Boys for the latter portion of his elementary school years. My parent's social status and Poppa's fast moving career finally afforded them the opportunity for one of us to attend private school.

"I think they were struggling with how to raise us as mixed race children," my brother said. He joined my critical thinking as we were trying to understand our parents' motives for trying to move us out of the District's public school system. "Cheryl, what would make Poppa think that they could have even made application for you back in December 1963 as a little colored girl?"

My brother scratched his head to imagine our parents' thought process decades ago. I was way too dedicated and independent to switch gears by the time they could afford private school. I think that my course was somewhat set in stone. I am sure they thought about whether raising us completely as black children without a complete regard for our diversity of culture, ethnicity or our racial admixtures was the best thing to do. Jefferson Junior High School was it for me, and I kept traveling down that black D.C. teen route into and through high school.

By the time I finally began attending junior high school, Momma's behavior became strange, and Poppa was advancing through politics rather well. Poppa was working for the United States Information Agency as an information officer at the time of our relocation. Many of Poppa's career photos were branded with a cigarette wedged between his fingertips; it was definitely the "Edward R. Murrow" look. Poppa smoked Winston cigarettes then switched to the 1956 Kent brand of the rich and famous. It was important for Poppa to project an image of being affluent. Upon receiving promotion after promotion, Poppa was called to evening affairs, business receptions, and special banquets. After-work hours became difficult for Momma, as she seemed cautious in leaving us with a sitter to attend Poppa's community affairs events. Poppa managed the stress of juggling, midnight runs to visit his family, our immediate family drama and his flourishing career.

Poppa could see himself appointed as Mayor to the District of Columbia after then-Mayor Walter Washington's tenure. This all happened before 1973 when Congress finally enacted the District of

Columbia Home Rule Act which provided for an elected mayor in place of the old system: a 13-member Council of the District of Columbia. Poppa was working hard to follow Walter Washington's mayoral footsteps. Feature articles in the newspaper with Poppa's name in the headline appeared more and more throughout the years. The people of D.C. were already beginning to acknowledge Poppa's climb to the top of both District and Federal Government career opportunities. Back and forth from the District to the U.S. Government departments and executive positions, Poppa was scaling up the super-grade ladder of success. The kitchen table was always our conference space for Poppa bringing home his new job promotions.

"Norma look, look. Cheryl, Chico, come look. I'm in the newspaper," Poppa announced running into the house after receiving a copy of January 1965's *The Washington Informer*. He'd been featured on the headline having received yet another promotion. Our kitchen table might as well have been a conference table surrounded by a dozen of Poppa's applauding peers.

"Look, Norma, they're announcing my new job." The article's opening paragraph read:

"Horace Holmes, 38, has been selected Program Analyst in the Program Coordinating Unit, Department of General Administration, District Government was effective December 21, 1964."

On the front page of the *Washington Informer,* Poppa appeared in his own branded style. He was holding tilted papers in his left hand, a gold Cross pen wedged between his fingers as if always ready for writing, a tailored suit furnished with a thin strip-striped tie, a gold watch cresting through his starch cuffed shirt sleeves, and his gold wedding band.

"Folks, I will have to work a little harder and won't be home for dinner some nights. Cheryl, go easy on your mother for me. OK, baby? Be a good girl for Poppa," Poppa said. I offered no response. "Cheryl, do you hear me? I need you to work with your Momma. No back talk, do you hear me young lady?"

"Yes, Poppa," I answered, with a 'but you don't understand what I am going through' heartfelt cry of turmoil.

The bottom half of the front page featured a full photo of President Johnson, Lady Bird, and Hubert Humphrey with his wife Muriel at a grand state reception, yet Poppa had received news priority over them. The article continued to highlight his upwardly mobile steps from his humble beginnings at Dunbar High School through his Juvenile Court appointment to his United States Information Agency career onward to the District Department of General Administration. Our family dinner table was the gathering spot for Poppa's regular job status reports. That is just what Poppa was about: jobs, getting jobs, and making sure the community had jobs.

Momma drifted behind the scenes in mine and Poppa's social lives. Being the exotic woman on my father's fraternity arm was a little different than being a political wife. Momma did appear when it was necessary and politically correct. Besides that, she wanted to remain in the background.

"You know Cheryl, we had to have background checks every six months because of our State Department work and Federal Government careers," Aunt June told me after I'd reached adulthood. "We were constantly under surveillance. Your mother and I would always talk, even laugh about our telephone calls being tapped. I really think your mother didn't want to draw any attention as your father's career was advancing."

I think Aunt June was right, and that Momma didn't want Poppa to be rejected because of her questionable racial status. Interracial marriage was very taboo and very illegal in most states until 1967. It was even more questionable in the Maryland and Virginia counties all around us. It's possible that Momma began to realize she was somewhat a hindrance to me socially, as well. She disappeared from the social aspect of my life for my benefit. My friends knew I had a mother, but she was almost invisible. I think Momma took some type of martyrdom approach to step back from my life so that I might enjoy being a black teen. I've carried guilt over that for a lifetime.

The move to 16th Street did have its benefits for me. Hustling and traveling through the city transit systems made me more independent, and the affluent lifestyle exposure forced me to strive for acceptance in Poppa's world of Washington's Negro bourgeoisie. A typical day's work for Momma would end with an evening of dinner and watching the soap operas she had recorded while at work. Momma multitasked making her island crafts such as quilts, crocheting, knitting, sewing, cutting recipes and solving crossword puzzles while watching the soap operas. In addition to making her island crafts, Momma would read romance novels and write letters to Granny Sabino. This was how she passed the time when she was living on the islands, and she kept those activities alive in her D.C. lifestyle. Little Chico sat at Momma's footstool, playing with little army men and tiny box cars he stored in a shoebox. Poppa was either in his office preparing for his next day's work, a keynote banquet speech at banquets or attending evening board meetings. I could be found in my room with the door closed by myself.

"Norma, please try with Cheryl. Isn't there anything that you can find to do so you can have something in common," Poppa asked Momma. If Poppa's master plan was in priority form, then keeping his family together and happy was at the top.

"Ma'an (man or mon), Cher'rell is...I cay'ant get her interested in anything, Horace. She just isn't interested. I'm at a loss, ma'an. She just doesn't want anything I have to offer her."

"But you just can't stay wrapped up in Horace Jr., Norma. You have two children."

"She only listens to you and only wants you. What am I supposed to do with that? There's no use with this, Horace. She just doesn't want me around."

Momma tried teaching me how to crochet and needle point. Lawdy, I was a D.C. girl, what would I do with doilies and needle point plaques? She tried to teach me how to sew which was a disaster. She tried teaching me to cook and bake; I really couldn't get the hang of it. We just couldn't find common ground. I had lost my routine of wandering around my Northeast neighborhood like a homeless child looking for a pseudo-mother. There were no friends to make so walks around the blocks were fruitless. I wanted a mother-daughter relationship, but I had been emotionally abandoned. Momma was nowhere to be found, and when she was, my baby brother was glued to her side. This new 16th street neighborhood was harrowing, cold and sterile.

My afternoons gave way to watching American Bandstand and D.C.s new Negro community outreach project for African American teens, the "Teenarama Dance Show." In "Hair Spray"-like nostalgia, I became enthralled with Washington's phenomena of hand-dancing. Practicing my moves for hours became my new solitary activity. I saved my allowance money and collected 45 R.P.M. Motown hits. Even if stopping at the downtown record stores on the way home from Southwest D.C. became a weekly routine, Poppa steered me away from what were regarded as "hangin' out" activities. I was watching the community's African-American youth dancing from afar, because the WOOK TV 14 television station where the dancing happened was off-limits. That didn't stop me from being a star in my bedroom in front of the mirror.

To keep busy during the summers, Poppa got me a work permit and made a few phone calls. When I was around 14-ish, I met Jerri, the Assistant Director of Cultural Activities for the D.C. Department of Recreation. She was my first real boss, and I would work for her during all of my summers through high school and college. As her career progressed, Jerri became the Director of the D.C. Department of Recreation. Jerri had a gift for dealing with children. We traveled all over Washington, D.C. visiting neighborhood recreation centers with a cultural awareness puppet show, "Puppets With A Purpose." She took me to every playground alleyway and city corridor where one could find D.C. youth congregating.

"I thought you were playing 'black'," Jerri told me recently. "I assumed you were compensating for not being completely black and were trying so much to fit in." Amazed at her comments, I had to take her reflections seriously.

"No Jerri, I didn't know I wasn't all black. I really didn't know."

"When you were a teenager, I knew you were part Asian even before I met your mother. Didn't you know you weren't all black? Just looking at yourself and looking at your mom, didn't you know you were of mixed, mixed blood?"

Jerri came to the Mid Atlantic area from Oklahoma. Growing up within the Oklahoma mixes of white, black and Amerindian, she could spot someone of mixed race with ease. With her own family members having chosen to acclimate to a variety of racial genres, mixed blood issues were an everyday occasion for her. It was the term "*mixed blood*" that caught my attention. Jerri's words challenged my thinking about how ignorant I'd been about my race as a youth. After all these years of a relationship, she finally expressed her earnest reflections about my childhood.

"Cheryl, I thought you were trying hard to be accepted. Your clothes, your speech, your manner...I thought you were compensating for not being black. I really thought you knew you were mixed and were trying to fit in socially with the other black teens."

"Jerri, why didn't you tell me," I asked, holding back tears.

"I thought you knew," she replied in further amazement.

Membership and acceptance into the Alpha Kappa Alpha sororal organization, the Girlfriends, the Links women's social clubs, and Jack and Jill of America, Inc. were "must needs" for social inclusion in the 60's. Membership into these networks were the high marks of status in the Washington, D.C. Negro world's social radar screen labeling you as a part of the upper crust Negro community. Jack and Jill of America Inc., the best of these social groups, was an exclusive Negro mothers club designed to bring the finest local Negro children together for fostering social and cultural relationships. Today, mothers of any race are allowed, but membership still requires sponsorship from a mother who is already in the group. The Washington, D.C. chapter was the third chapter club organized in 1940. Momma wasn't a member either by choice or racial exclusion.

I had to have the correct answers to some important questions to be regarded as a fit for this new social kingdom.

"What's your last name?"

"Where does your father work?"

"Is your father a doctor?"

"Do you live on 16th Street?"

"How high up on 16th Street do you live?"

"Did you go to Mrs. Howard's Nursery School?"

"Do you have a house at Highland Beach?"

"Do you get your hair done at Cardozo Sisters?"

"Do you take dance lessons at the Jones- Haywood School of Ballet?"

"Do you take music lessons at Howard University?"

"Does your father have a low tag number?"

"How low is his tag number?"

"Are you related to the real estate Holmes family?"

"Do you go to St. Luke's Church?"

These were qualifying questions needing exclusive answers, and if correct, they granted passage into D.C.'s finest Negro fiefdoms. I wanted to become friends with my fellow princess daughters. Every new opportunity for making friends opened with this tribunal line of questioning. They were like bullets to the heart piercing every vessel, particularly if you had an incorrect answer.

There was one question that trumped all the rest:

"Are you in Jack and Jill?"

I could never answer, and that lack of an answer kept me out of the 1960's D.C. black teen in-crowd. I am not sure how "in it, yet not of it" would've been an answer. The pressure of fitting in as a Northwest Uptown Girl was a real nightmare. I do thank the few faithful among Poppa's friends who made sure I was included in all the Jack and Jill activities. There was one qualifier I possessed on my own merit: I am way lighter than a brown paper bag. There was an unspoken fair skin color code of acceptance, you know.

Poppa's social status made me halfway acceptable, and Momma's lack of social status put me halfway to nowhere in the scheme of our new environment. Poppa made sure I had everything needed to be accepted as an uptown black bourgeois Girl. I would soon have a car, trendy clothes, a telephone, and an uptown house. I had everything a young lady could want—except for my mother. There was just no explaining who Momma was, what her race was, why she was MIA, why she spoke so funny, and who all those assorted folks in the living room cocktail table were.

I could only make my social life half of what I wanted it to be because I had only half of the acceptable answers.

Honestly, that's the mixed race issue. You are not one race or the other; you are something different racially altogether. "Ya cay'aan't take da cream out of ya coffee after it's been stirred," as Momma would say.

I thought I was just like every other African-American, Washington, D.C. teenager. All I ever wanted, was to dance on the Teenarama Dance show. I never thought differently. Photo: Beverly Lindsay-Johnson, *Dance Party: The Teenarama Story.*

HAIR

On Saturday nights, Momma would wash my hair following a routine of toweling it, parting it, combing it, and oiling it. My hair, not being of any particular texture, was difficult to groom and style. One part straight, one part curly and one part nappy—it's tri-textual. Momma would use Brylcreem, a white man's hair pomade created in 1928 by County Chemicals, to slick out, smooth, and straighten my hair.

She did realize that my hair was too sensitive for WD-40 hair pomades and found that lighter hair grooming products like Vitapoint and V05 worked better than heavy-duty Ultra Sheen solutions. Even today, I struggle to keep my ends meeting properly. I make my own hair grease with "lite" pomades made of mineral oil, Vaseline, glycerin and water. My hair needs just a light touch in order to be tamed. Momma liked Brylcreem more than anything else on the market though.

In Audre Lorde's autobiographical narrative *Zami; A New Spelling of My Name,* she describes the experience of Momma's Saturday night living room beauty parlor:

"I remember the warm mother smell caught between her legs, and the intimacy of our physical touching nestled inside of the anxiety/pain like a nutmeg nestled inside its covering of mace."

It's every little black girl's journey with Momma and hair, even little girls with mixed roots. With every pull of the curl and every snag of my wavy endings, I envied Momma's Filipina hair. "God, why don't I have hair like Momma's," was my every waking thought.

Momma used half a tube of Brylcreem each week, and then cocked a flower on the side of my head like I was in the islands. The weekend's arduous task of doing my hair made things even more complicated between us, as Momma had a baby daughter with mixed roots, and all of them were in my head. Let us not forget that Momma was trying to figure out her own perfect head of hair in America, too.

Poppa had to call me out of my upstairs hiding place on some hair nights. "Cheryl, where are you? Come on shuggie, your Momma wants to do your hair."

"No. I don't want her to do my hair. She doesn't understand what it feels like. I don't look like her. She doesn't know what she's doing. She and Chico have hair the same. Why did I get hair like this? It's not fair, it's just not fair," I shouted down the stairs.

"Don't talk about your Momma like that."

"Poppa, I want hair like Momma. Why don't I have hair like Momma. It's not fair, Poppa. Why am I made this way? Poppa, I don't understand."

"Honey, I know, but Momma has to wash your hair tonight. Do it for me. I love you so much. Please, just go and try not to cry. I love you just the way you are. I understand how you feel. Come here baby, give me a hug. I understand it hurts, but we have to do it. O.K.?

Give me a hug. You can do it. Be a big girl for me. Go and let Momma do your hair."

Crying before the comb even tackled every wave, curl, and knot, I stomped down the steps to Momma's lap with my lips poked out. Every Saturday was a reminder that something made me different than both of my parents. My head of hair made me feel like an outcast.

"Horace, what are we going to do with this child's head," Momma said. "It's not her hair that's the problem. It's her attitude, and it's her mouth. She is so rude that I can't control her. Horace, she hates me. The way she talks to me—she's so mad, Horace. I don't know what to do with her or this head of hair."

"Norma, I'll ask around. My sister says that The Cardozo Sisters do the best hair in the city."

Poppa was always collecting quid-pro-quo for his daughter. Anybody who wanted in on the executive side of government wanted and needed Poppa's friendship, and the quickest way to Horace Holmes Sr.'s heart was through his baby girl. Poppa really wanted to stay in front of any trouble I could run into on the field of life, unfortunately, the only trouble I had was right in my home. I was in the middle of a war with Momma, and Momma was in the middle of a war with Sadie. For Poppa's sake, many of his female friends would scoop me up and take me to social outings. Respectfully and empathetically they would always inquire, "How's your mother?"

The first time going to the hair salon was quite a family affair. Poppa, Momma and Baby Brother all marched me into the shop to get my plats cut off. The stylist first pulled the shearing clippers and the good ol' bottle of Vigorol hair relaxer treatment off of the shelf. Every little baby boomer "colored" chil' knows about the suffocating, egg smelling little bottle of liquid sulfur called a relaxer. You pour it on, let it sit, and pray for clemency. I don't really know if the stuff works or not, but it surely made me gag.

Poppa assisted in helping me succeed socially as best he could, but I needed a mother who herself was accepted on this Poppa's turf. Without Momma's participation or inclusion into this arena, it was virtually impossible for me to be accepted, too. Momma didn't want to have anything to do with Poppa's social circles at all. Those Jack and Jill Mothers who let me play with their little princesses were so mindful enough to ask, "How's your Mother? Give her my best," even if they didn't necessarily care how Momma was doing. Momma usually had the same reply to their greetings.

"Well, if they want to know about me, they can call me. Ma'an, they are awl-fon-nies," Momma would say, and suck in her teeth. Sticking her chin out and lifting her head high, she'd say "To hell with dem." Recently, I finally mustered up the courage to ask a truthful question of a childhood friend's mother, who was also a friend of my father.

"Did Jack and Jill not let my family in because of my mother," I asked my father's friend.

"Your mother wasn't social at all," my father's friend replied. "Whether she was asked to join or not, you know it all depended on your friendship with a sponsoring mother. Your father always called me to keep abreast of the activities and wanted you to be included."

For me to be accepted in this social melee, my mother needed to be fashionable, gregarious, savvy, aspiring, influential, and definitely a Negro woman. She was none of the above. Her fair complexion was not black or white, but yellow, if anything. Momma's hair was pin-straight and not straight from the Ultra Sheen box or from Madame C.J. Walker's pressing comb. I couldn't belong to anything that required my mother to be a savvy Negro mother, so I went alongside the social greats of the community riding on my father's name. I wanted to sit with my father at the D.C. head dais banquet table and would do it with or without Momma.

I would pray to tears, "Lord, I want to be in Jack and Jill, please." My parents would never explain our "acceptable yet unacceptable" status of exclusion.

Poppa was taking me to a Jack and Jill tween party one evening, and of course I was only an invited guest. We were standing at the front door ready to leave for the party, and I remember standing at the narthex of the new house.

"Why can't we be in Jack and Jill, Poppa?"

"Cheryl, we'll have to talk about that later. If you want to go, we'll have to hurry along. I promised to pick up a few of your friends."

Mangos don't fall far from the mango tree. A few of the Queen Mothers of this secret society treated Momma poorly, and their daughters were just as bad to me. Loneliness and rejection became my best friends while Momma and I kept spiraling downhill in our relationship. The older I got, the more contentious and frequent our arguments became. She would remind me during stressful arguments that my rudeness would cause her a sudden death.

"Ma'an, ya dus be full of rudeness. Ya mout gonna get ya in trouble meh'son," Momma said.

God finally answered my prayer, as I am a Jack and Jill Mother some forty-odd years later. Living in New England as I do now, Jack and Jill keeps our children well-exposed to the African-American social culture and helps to cultivate friendships. In my adult racial status of "passin' black," I had been sponsored into the club when my children were young. I've even been an executive board member on several occasions.

I have the right answer now.

I never completely understood our exclusion until I attended a recent board meeting.

"We are a mothers club. When we accept new members, they have to be referred. The basic requirement—when you suggest a mom for membership, you have to know them. We trust that they are your friends when you submit their name. You must know the mothers well in order to recommend them to our chapter," one of the board members explained. It was all news to me.

"So...am I clear to understand that membership is based on the relationship referrals of the sponsoring mother, and this is an African-American mothers club built on those relationships and those respective sponsoring referrals. You really only want membership suggested candidates from folk we know personally?"

"Yeah, Rev. You got it."

The entire board looked at me, nodded, and shook their heads to the affirmative.

I bowed my head, and warm tears ran from my eyes to my breast plate. The 1950s Jack and Jill club didn't want Momma, and Momma didn't want them either. Momma wasn't an African-American woman and wasn't a socialite friend to any of these D.C. chapter's mothers. Whichever way it really was, I was out of the game. All of Poppa's social, political and D.C. family's correct legacy couldn't make me completely fit in with Washington's Negro social elite.

My heart still fills up when my friends come to the Jack and Jill monthly meetings. Many of the moms are legacy members, i.e., they were childhood members who were "grandfathered" into the club as adults. Often, they walk into an evening meeting with their copies of "Up The Hill," the national yearly publication of the organization's regional graduating children and chapter highlights. If your childhood records of participation are lost for any reason, the publication proves your membership and that you were in the numbers of participation in your region. "Up The Hill" is your badge of honor. I always look for my picture in the background scenes of group shots. I am in a few, but I don't have legacy status. Can you believe it? My heart still weeps as I look for my face in the party scenes. Somewhere, one of the copies has my picture captured in the background. I was there, but not included. This was my teenage world "black in the day."

Momma started drifting back even more from my everyday life. She focused on Chico, and I was left to my room to hand-dance alone for hours at a time. Granny Sadie was off limits to the Holmes home by this time. For Thanksgiving 1965, we visited Granny Sadie one more time.

"I'm not going," I said, refusing one of the last attempts at a Holmes family dinner. I hated the red dress I was wearing, and Momma wouldn't let me take it off. That dress wasn't flattering, considering that I would soon be under inspection. My attitude was similar to Momma's at that point. I was tired of being stared at, picked at, and I was tired of the inevitable outcome of more family warfare.

"If Uncle Landon says I am fat one more time—I'm not going to that woman's house," I blurted. Chico was observing, now old enough to digest some our family's drama. I was descending down the stairs to the front door. Poppa, standing in front of me, whisked around and glared at me.

"Don't you ever talk about my mother like that again," Poppa warned.

"I don't care what you want me to do. I don't want to go."

All of a sudden, his right arm came up, and his right hand swung across my face. Poppa had back-handed me across my mouth; his revered Howard University class ring, now a pinkie ring, had clipped my mouth and chipped my lower-left front tooth. The chip is ever so small. There are moments, even now, that my tongue rolls over and rests along the top edge of my bottom front tooth. I feel the chip. I can't see the chip, but it now exists as a reminder of Sundays with Granny Sadie and my "mout full of rudeness." Dear God, the mention of her today still makes my brother hyperventilate. Sunday dinners would eventually dwindle down to Uncle Landon and Aunt Mary visits only until the Sunday before Poppa died.

I was advancing normally through my "tween" years at Jefferson Jr. High School as my National Cathedral Girls School regard fizzled. Jefferson Jr. High School offered the same academic magnet school exposure as offered by Amidon Elementary. I entered art contests, and worked in the summers using my art talents. Poppa insisted that I acquire a strong base of academic skills in case I didn't succeed in my desires for an art career. He wanted to make sure I had a backup plan.

"Cheryl, you always have to have a plan. From the time I was eleven years old I was working to take care of myself and to go to school," Poppa told me as a tween. "After I passed the civil service exam, I was sixteen when I got my first typing job. I kept saving for college, and kept going to school until I finished graduate school. Cheryl, I even applied to Georgetown law school. I was going to attend, but your brother was born. I needed to work and Momma needed help with the two of you. You have to have a plan to succeed, and I know you will. Cheryl, make your plan. And I want you to stop arguing with your Momma."

"Alright Poppa, I understand. I really want to go to Art College. I will figure it out with my art teachers. I will come back with a plan," I assured Poppa.

"Have you discussed this with Momma? Just don't argue with her, O.K., pun'kin?"

"No," I replied. "No."

One Valentine's Day at school pretty much explains what I was going through. I brought in Valentines for everyone I could remember, but no one remembered me. "Baby, they are just jealous," Poppa said to me. I could never figure that one out, because I had nothing to be jealous of. The Lord became my dearest friend from that moment forward.

The years continued moving along the exact course without change and uneventfully in the same manner. Poppa kept steadily moving up the Government executive ladder: GS 7s, 9s, 12s and into the GS-teens where no black man traveled. Momma was becoming more reserved with each of his career advancements.

We still weren't allowed to see Granny Sadie, and Chico stayed near Momma's hip. The Margaret M. Amidon Magnet School curriculum that applied to Junior High School had run its course and ended upon my graduation from Jefferson Junior High School. The D.C. public schools abolished their track system, and everyone from around Washington, no matter the academic program, was required to return to their neighborhood school. In 1967, I was reassigned to my neighborhood high school, Calvin Coolidge High School. In 1968, Poppa got a really big job which he announced at our kitchen conference table.

Poppa lit up a cigarette before sitting down to make his latest announcement.

"Norma, Willard Wirtz offered me a new job. I have to take it. I have to take it for us, for everyone, Norma. For everyone–Norma, I have to take it." Poppa realized that he'd been placed on a mantle of responsibility for all Negroes in our city. He was one big step closer to having it all, and it had all gone according to his planning.

"I'm going to be the first D.C. Manpower Administrator appointed from the U.S. Department of Labor. It also means I will be a member of Walter Washington's Cabinet. Norma, I will be on the Mayor's Cabinet, too. It's a real big job, kids. Next stop, the Mayor's Office."

"Poppa, what does that mean?" I asked him.

"I'm going to help make jobs for people, honey. Cheryl, it's going to mean a lot of community work after my work hours. I will be out at meetings and community events in the evening in order to do my job. People need jobs, and I am going to give a lot of people work so they can earn a living. Try to understand baby, O.K.?"

Poppa wasn't finished.

"You know Cheryl, it's time for you to grow up a little, try for me. Just try to get along with Momma when I'm not here, O.K. honey?"

He faced Momma.

"Norma, we can do this. I sure hope you will be able to come out with me like you used to. The children will be fine; we'll find a sitter in the evening." Poppa unfolded a variety of D.C. newspapers and clippings. Poppa's promotion was plastered all over the D.C. newspapers and Negro tabloids. "Washington Gets Unique Centralized Agency on Manpower, Washington, D.C., Friday, March 22, 1968," Poppa read *The Evening Star* headlines aloud.

"Horace, I'll do what I can. You know the children come first, and your mother isn't an option any longer for watching the children," was Momma's reply to Poppa's big news. "We'll figure it out as we go along. Congratulations, baby."

I was sixteen then, and with a little extra cash from his GS-17 promotion, Poppa taught me to drive and then gave me a set of my very own wheels. I enjoyed the freedom that a new car gave me and frequented the new boutiques and hippie shops in Georgetown. The ol' Foggy Bottom and Negro Georgetown, were gentrifying and becoming trendy. Shops were beginning to line up and down

Wisconsin Avenue and across M. St. N.W. The criss-cross intersection was becoming busy and the streetcar tracks and cobblestone streets made going on that side of town a bumpy road but worth the trip. Tattered row houses were being converted to posh townhouse urban flats and resold to those who could carry their high-priced mortgages. Blacks were moving out and whites were moving in, leaving no room for even the simplest of street parking. Finding a space for your car in Georgetown was a rarity. An afternoon in Georgetown was and is still worth the trip in spite of the congestion and headache from hustling about the area.

I liked to shop by myself. The trendy vogue denim jean stores were my favorite Georgetown shops and down the street was the start of a new concept in town: the Unisex Hair Salon. I dared to visit not knowing if they could tackle my crazy tri-textural, mixed rooted head of hair.

Oh, my hair. Those Cardozo Sisters tried everything they knew to do. They set it, they rolled it, they hot ironed, they hot curled it, they shish-kabobed it. They experimented using every process they knew to find a working combination for my mixed-rooted hair. I have a strand from each race that I am mixed with: black, white, Amerindian and Asian. If there were going to be any more experiments on my head, I was going to take matters into my own hands. I needed to go to the Dominican shops because they were better-suited for working with a blended head of hair. Ironically, the suggestion to go to a Dominican shop was advice given to Momma for her hair—she wouldn't go. I was so indoctrinated that I was racially black that there was nothing in my world's perspective that could ever suggest or would make me think that anyone in a trendy white Georgetown hair salon could do my hair. Momma couldn't help me with it anymore, either. I'll never forget the day I walked into the salon and dared to pop the question to the receptionist.

"Can I...I mean, are you able to do my hair?"

To my absolute surprise, her answer was "Yes, do you want an appointment now?"

The shops were walk-in. I remember that it was a white hairstylist, my first, who showed me how to do my hair.

Wash, blow dry and bump with an electric curling iron on a medium to low setting.

I learned to stir fry my hair with a light toss. I felt that if I actually had hair like Momma's everyone wouldn't stare so much at us. "Who is that child with that beautiful woman," people were saying to themselves, I was certain of it. Momma had beautiful straight Asian locks and my mixed roots made me feel so badly out of place. I just wanted to feel like I was my mother's child. My hair was a dead giveaway that maybe Momma wasn't my mother. Well, Momma had tried her best and took me as far as she could go. A new car and Georgetown took me the rest of the way especially when it came to hair styling and maintenance.

Now in high school, I followed suit with the other teens as we all explored the wonderful world of dating.

"Lord, I want a real boyfriend," I prayed. Already, I was thinking a man would solve all my problems.

METRO AREA

The Evening Star

Washington Gets Unique Centralized Agency on Manpower

Poppa was always in the news, accomplishment after accomplishment. Bottom left: Poppa pictured with Mayor Walter Washington, Secretary of Labor Willard Wirtz, 1968. Bottom right: always by his side, Uncle Jack pictured with Maria Hodgson, wife of Secretary of Labor James Hodgson, 1970 and Dr. Bennetta B. Washington, wife of Mayor Walter Washington.

DEATH'S CALL

Poppa's work was beginning to bear fruit around the city, and Poppa would be recognized for it. The door bell rang while we were at Poppa's kitchen conference table in 1969. I ran to answer.

"Ma'an ask who it 'tis," Momma shouted.

"Yeah, Ma, yeah—" I said, and I sucked my teeth as I often did at Momma's quirky phobias. I opened the door.

"Here little lady, give this to your daddy," the man said, giving me a little brown envelope.

"Poppa, it's for you," I said. He'd later let us read the news.

"Mr. Holmes, it is our pleasure to inform you that you have been selected to receive the 1969 Howard University Alumni Achievement Award for your contribution in Labor and Public Service. Please reply via telegram of your acceptance and appearance at the Howard University Charter Day Dinner, which further commemorates the university's One Hundred and Second Anniversary. Congratulations, Mr. Holmes for receiving the Alumni Charter Day Award of Howard University for Distinguished Post Graduate Achievement; please reply via a collect telegraph whether you will accept."

"Horace, that's wonderful. Where is it going to be held," Momma asked, quite pleased that the event was sponsored by her alma mater.

"Norma, it looks like it's going to be held at the Washington Hilton in the International Ballroom. You will be coming with me, won't you?"

"Yes, Horace."

"Poppa, can I go—please, can I go too," I asked.

"No honey, you will have to stay home with Chico, but I will be sure to bring you the program and tell you all about it. You just be a good little girl for Poppa, O.K.? No trouble out of you, this is real important for your mother and me. I need you to work with us." Poppa was hoping I wouldn't have some type of attention-getting behavioral attack or outburst argument with Momma which might've given his dear wife a reason not to attend.

Poppa kept good company that evening alongside five of Howard University's finest alumni. The following day's *The Washington Post* morning headline read, "*Five Honored At Charter Day Dinner.*" The photo was accompanied by the caption reading:

Alumni Achievement Award Recipients (from left to right) Horace R. Holmes, The Reverend Kelly Miller Smith, Dr. Bennetta B. Washington, Mr. Harris L. Woffard, Jr. and The Reverend Andrew J. Young.

Poppa was flying high and had no idea of the crash landing ahead.

Life is poetic, so poetic justice rules every corner of our living. Poppa wanted me to be an overachiever like him, to be empowered, independent, and always-aspiring just in case Prince Charming never appeared.

"You must be independent. You must be able to take care of yourself. Be prepared," Poppa would rehearse his wisdom mantras over and over. His words of wisdom were very well-received in my heart. However, bizarre as it may seem, it was Momma's advice that always prevailed over Poppa's. He invited me into his office library.

"Cheryl, have you been thinking about where you would like to go for college after high school? Cheryl do you have your plan set? Remember?" I was always a little hesitant about sharing my deepest desire, but I had the courage to tell him the truth.

"Poppa, I want to be an artist. You know, ever since Auntie Rita gave me my first oil painting set, I have wanted to be an artist. I want to go to art school, and I know that's not a liberal arts background, but I really want to try. I wasn't sure what you would think, so I haven't said much about college."

"Cheryl, I will pay for anything you want to study. If you want to study art than study art. Whatever you want to do, just be the best black woman in America you can be. That's the only thing I require; just be the best one in the field. Understand, Cheryl?"

"Yes, Poppa," I said. Maybe Poppa saw it and maybe he didn't, but I sighed in relief. "Just like I promised, I have done some research and I know you want to make sure I have an academic degree. There is this type of school called art college, which means I can study art and still earn a Bachelors of Fine Arts degree. I'd like to apply to the Rhode Island School of Design, Pratt Institute and Boston University–just to be on the safe side. Can I Poppa?"

"Cheryl, as long as you are studying and moving to the top of your area of interest, I will be pleased with your choice. Start writing your requests for catalogs and applications and you can use my office and typewriter over the file cabinet," Poppa said, and I remember the joy in his tone. A lit cigarette was curled between his fingers. "You know baby, you won't be like my mother, you won't be like my sister and you won't be like your mother. Get all the knowledge you can, Cheryl. That's the only thing they can't take away from you." By that point in my young womanhood, I could understand exactly what Poppa was talking about.

Decades later, I remember laughing to myself in one of my first seminary classes with the acclaimed Womanist Theologian, Delores Williams. We were studying about the genre of African-American Religions. She was pontificating about Alice Walker and the term "womanish," thusly, the origins of Womanist Theology. Womanist Theology is juxtaposing women of color voices to Feminist Christology. Jacquelyn Grant explains it all in her book title, "White Women's Christ and Black Women's Jesus;" the title alone speaks volumes to how women can view the cultural perspective of Jesus Christ from their own lenses.

My goodness, Poppa raised me as a Womanist; tell me something I don't know.

Momma ensured my future in her own way. She may have not been able to figure out the African-American lifestyle, but she figured out life. Momma gave me her best dose of wisdom, and only the Lord knows why I finally listened to her.

"Cher' rell, don't bring anything less than your father in this house. He has to be better looking than your father and able to make more money than your father. If he doesn't fit that picture frame, don't bring him in here to me, ma'an," Mrs. Norma Sabino Holmes would say on a regular basis. These were her only words that I truly ever obeyed wholeheartedly; all was not lost with Momma. Momma knew that eventually I was going to want it all, plus a man and a family. She knew how to pick men for me, too. For her, it was just as easy as picking men the opposite of her father. That was her standard: marry someone better than any crappy father which life could have thrown your way. I had a great dad, so I'd have to say that her eye for men was pretty good.

Momma's words rang true when God orchestrated an unbelievable plan for me to meet Phillip, my high school's senior class president at Calvin Coolidge High. Talk about one answered prayer—the year our families met, the gregarious young Phillip was a great student, and had even won Washington's popular hand dance contest. From the moment Momma met Phillip she adored him, just like I did.

The Historic Howard Theatre at D.C.s corner of 7th and T Streets, Northwest Washington was known for providing entertainment to an African-American audience for decades until the riots after Martin Luther King's 1968 assassination occurred. The theatre hosted many of the great early and mid-20th century black musical artists, comedy acts and theatrical plays. By the 1970s, since the theatre had experienced such damage from the riots, it became difficult to repair, restore and maintain; it closed in 1970. There were many attempts toward revival through the 70s and 80s. It finally reopened in 2012 as a local historical landmark and a brand new artist facility. The Howard Theatre's restoration project brings hope for its future as the corner is quite an international gathering spot. Similar in perception to Harlem's Apollo Theatre in the New York City Negro community, the Howard Theatre was referred to as the "largest colored theatre in the world." The Howard Theatre was founded in 1910 and was billed as the "Theater of the People." I still remember Poppa taking me to the Howard Theatre for the first time on a Saturday afternoon.

"Poppa, why does that man keep coming back with a different cape on," I asked the first time I saw James Brown perform which was quite fascinating. "Why is he falling all over the floor? Isn't the show over?"

Poppa loved taking me to the Howard Theatre, but Momma had the top-of-the-chart view for every show that came in town. Traditionally, all of the acts in town at the Howard Theatre for performing would pause their schedules to entertain the students at Howard University. The Howard University Auditorium would receive any and all of the acts in town as a part of their menu of student activities. I could depend on Momma always bringing home free tickets to some of the best shows in town. Oh my goodness, my favorite was the Motortown Revue, Motown's packaged —"chitlin' circuit" tour featuring The Marvelettes, Martha and the Vandellas, The Contours, The Temptations, The Supremes and Little Stevie Wonder with his harmonica. My absolute favorite occasion at the theatre was when Smokey Robinson and The Miracles, sang with his wife Claudette. Best of all, Momma would bring home free tickets to any or all of the shows in town just for me.

"Cher'rell, ma'an, I got eight tickets to see Nancy Wilson here, ma'an, go."

"Eight tickets, that's a lot," I thought to myself. I could really have a party with eight free tickets for the next evening's performance on campus. "Wow, Momma. Thanks." I was very moved that she handed over the tickets. I called everyone I could think of to invite, and can you believe it, not one person was available to go. I will always remember standing in my father's library that late afternoon before the show and calling her at work in order to return the tickets.

"Momma, I have to give you back the tickets. I don't have anyone to go with."

"Ma'an, dun't ya know a young ma'an you can invite?" She was actually empowering me to ask a boy out on a date. I couldn't believe it. "Think about it ma'an, I know you have a young man you can ask."

"Momma, I don't know anyone," I replied, even though something down deep was saying, "Don't miss your opportunity." I had been around the senior class planning committees trying to decide what initiative I wanted to help out with. Phillip had been organizing all of the activities, but I only knew him from the student graduation planning meetings. I dared to find his home number and call him.

Phillip was over 6 feet tall and one sharp, handsome, light-skinned mulatto young man. He always smelled divine. He doused himself daily with splashes of the 1970s favorite male cologne Aramis. Two dabs behind each ear was just the right amount to notice his presence, and he had a crazy habit of dabbing the cologne under his nose and over his moustache. I suppose it was to leave the memory of his juicy kiss lingering. Clean-shaven with a scored out hairline, any little princess would adore his wavy hair and crystal clear light brown tiger eyes that glistened enchantment. He was a cavalier dresser, much like my father. I had no idea how finding this young man to escort me to a show would impact my life.

"Phillip, this is Cheryl Holmes. Listen, my mother has given me some free tickets to see Nancy Wilson perform on Howard's campus for the student body. Would you like to go? The show is tonight."

"Sure, let me call my mother and I will call you right back," my prince said. He called back a few minutes later. "Cheryl, I can go but my mother works at night and I don't have a car." I was going to have to drive, and the entire situation made me real uncomfortable because this was so out of my mother's character to suggest that I become assertive about dating. Regardless, I followed through on that one date. After our evening together, we became good friends and started dating regularly.

We had found each other on our own terms, not realizing that a "priming of the well" plan had already happened behind the scenes. A member of Phillip's church actually worked with Momma at the student health services clinic. Mrs. Phifer had been trying to play cupid.

"Norma, my deceased Pastor's son would be a nice young man for Cheryl; his wife is my best friend. I would like to introduce them," Mrs. Phifer told Momma. The good Lord ordered our footsteps so that we would actually meet at school. We discovered that Momma and Mrs. Phifer were actually trying to put us together; Momma had no idea that the young man who escorted me to the show was, in fact, Mrs. Phifer's select beau for me. Such serendipity—I felt it was a miraculous confirmation of our divine meeting. It was a sign from Heaven. From my mother's out of character behavior, to a godly coincidence of more than a chance meeting, I had no idea that the Lord was taking care of me to what would be the shockwave of my life, cascading into my future. I was going to love, value and need this young man then and even into my destiny; Phillip has been on a godly assignment to love me.

Phillip and I pretty much had a Barbie and Ken 1970 senior high school year. We had a wonderful academic school year of work, fun, and senior student activities.

Most exciting was Phillip's vision for our class's graduation to be held at the Great Crossing in the National Cathedral. I went and accompanied him to a site visit for planning the ceremony, and there I met a young rector, John Walker. Father Walker handled the scheduling calendar for the Cathedral. He gave us a tour of the church grounds and handled all of the details for the graduation. We were closing our tour and my mind began to imagine what it would be like to marry in the Cathedral's sanctuary and at its Great Crossing.

"Father Walker, although I am a member of St. Luke's Church, will you marry me here at the Cathedral?"

"I will. Just contact me when you are ready," Father Walker replied. The graduation was indeed held at the Washington National Cathedral as envisioned. It was unprecedented for our school to have the graduation ceremony off campus, and that is the legacy my graduating class leaves behind. It was our senior prom which spoke volumes to our mixed race family struggles. Phillip and I were a fine couple at our senior prom. Momma made my dress; I must say I was very *cutie pretty-ish.* I had developed into quite a Black American Princess. Phillip was his usual dashing self, and I was pretty cute in a floral gown—I had altered the pattern design myself. Momma was a seamstress and created the gown for me. We were quite the couple. If the graduation ceremony was being planned in grandiose fashion, you can imagine how the prom setting had been planned. The Indian Springs Country Club in Silver Spring, MD was the beautiful setting for quite a memorable senior prom occasion. Phillip's strategy was to provide the best of everything that living-large,-black high school students could afford. Nothing was too good for us, as the student government did its best to give us memories to last a lifetime.

It's time for me to mention the prom band. Now, Phillip and I were sashaying about the dance floor and winning over the crowd. I looked over at the band. My eye caught the eye of the lead vocalist; he looked like my first paternal cousin. I wasn't quite sure if it was him as I hadn't seen my paternal family members that much since Momma and the rest of us became disenfranchised with them.

"Phillip, I think that's my first cousin over there," I said, pointing to the gentleman in the band.

"Really? Go on over and see for sure," Phillip said. I walked over to get a closer look.

"Hi," I paused while losing my breath. "Are you my cousin?"

"Yes, you are Cousin Cheryl aren't you?" Mercy, it was my father's nephew, Aunt Thelma's son; Thelma was Poppa's sister.

My paternal first cousin was a vocalist and always had his heart set on becoming a Gospel singer. To my knowledge, he made only one album and every time I saw him around town with the same album clutched under his arm, he always tried to sell it to me. I could hear

Momma whispering in my head, "Be careful, those are your father's people, don't have anything to do with them. They don't want you. Just stay away from Granny Sadie and her clan."

By the time I was seventeen years old, staying away from my father's family was the only thing we could do to have a peaceful home. Here I am, at my senior prom, apprehensive of speaking to my paternal first cousin. What a shame. I grew up with no intimate day-to-day family relationships around me. My maternal family was an ocean apart, and honestly, I didn't know them very well. Special events, well-financed vacations, and weekly phone calls are all that we shared together.

I cherished every moment of the first year Phillip and I spent together. The closing year of high school kept us happy, busy, and elated with the expectancy of a bright future into young adulthood. Phillip went south to Atlanta for college and I headed to Providence to attend the Rhode Island School of Design.

Selecting a design college to attend was somewhat of a difficult decision, as all of my friends were seeking Ivy Group placements. We were the first generation with opportunities after the Civil Rights Movement. Discovering design college was a great solution for Poppa's demand for academics. I could attend college while studying my special interest. This was a win-win situation for me; it would please Poppa, and it would satisfy my desire to train as a corporate communications designer. Having grown up around Howard's campus, I opted for a brand new experience of leaving Poppa's black world. I ventured off to the brand new horizon of New England, but Poppa's world never left me in my heart or my thinking. It didn't take me long to become homesick for D.C., miserable without Poppa, and longing for Phillip. I couldn't see the light of a new racial scenario and its possibilities all around me. Of course, I made friends with all of the black students and the few black girls who entered my freshman class with me. I labeled myself on familiar ground. I was one of several black students to have been recruited into the school after the Civil Rights Movement.

As those revered Ivy Group colleges opened their affirmative action doors to the black community, so did the Rhode Island School of Design. I was in the numbers of those who gained admission to the prestigious art college.

"I hate to welcome you with this disclaimer, but half of you will not graduate," the freshman class official greeter told us.

"Well, you aren't speaking to me; I will finish," I said so that no one could hear me.

She was suggesting that the course of study was so very rigorous that many wouldn't be able to meet the challenge of successfully completing the program. During those preliminary weeks of the academic year, there were a lot of tears shed.

I had never been around so many white folks in my life. I thought white folks were just white folks until Nancy, one of my dorm mates, received a care package of Rosh Hashanah and Yom Kippur traditional foods, breads and little desserts. With glee, she shared how her mother had prepared everything for the Jewish Holidays and sent her a sample package.

"Doesn't everyone celebrate Christmas," I *actually* said. I had been so acculturated and indoctrinated as a Negro, I didn't realize that there were any other folks in the world. I had no real regard for other cultures, traditions, religions or races. I was diversely deprived. Poppa just wanted to make sure that I could scale the rough side of the black mountain and be able to stand on top and shout, "Here I am world, take it or leave it. I am here."

I was racially insulated in Washington. In D.C., the white folks ran America and the black folks ran D.C. and that was it. White folks would be on one side of the park, black folks on the opposite side. When Poppa taught me how to survive and maneuver around D.C., he forgot to mention there was a big melting pot outside of his hometown. Finding myself a little Afro-centric in the midst of such an Anglo New England was quite a culture shock. Even more of a shock was the first young man who came to ask me out for a date.

"You can't go out with him, he's white."

All of my black student union girl friends gathered around me to make sure I was in my right mind. A young robber-baron-surnamed gentleman had become interested in getting to know me. I was very intrigued as to why he was curious about getting to know me; of course my cadre from the sistah-hood gave me sound counsel.

"Why do you think he is interested in me," I asked and was confident my sistah-hood Sanhedrin-like Council had insight on a possible motive.

"Well, he is curious what it would be like to be with a black woman." They whole-heartedly convinced me to not date him just because he was white. I didn't want to date him only because I was completely devoted to Phillip. I still can't imagine what that white guy wanted with me. Now that I look back at it all, maybe he didn't even know I was black. I am sure he knew I wasn't completely black, or I was just black enough to test drive his curiosity about black women, because I look more white than I do black. Who knows what he was thinking, but it was the first time a white guy ever took an interest in me. It was more or less the first time I had been around any white young men anyway.

It didn't matter who else came along. Phillip was my boyfriend, eternally. I had made my decision. The bright future of college, having a long distance relationship, and being too young for a committed relationship was not changing my decision about Phillip. I was going to see what the future would hold for Mr. Miller and me. I had fallen in love with Phillip, and all I could hear was the 1960s female soul vocal group, Brenda and the Tabulations, offer sound advice from their hit titled, "Stay Together Young Lovers."

By 1970, Poppa had become that executive governmental Robin Hood figure he always wanted to be. He was a liaison between the Labor Department and the D.C. local government, which had an impact on jobs in the community. Poppa was truly "the Manpower Czar" as the Administrator of the District Manpower Administration, The Chairman of the Mayor's Manpower Advisory Committee, and a member of the President's Committee on Youth Opportunities. His list of professional affiliations was endless.

In 1970, I was determined to catch an Allegheny Airlines flight to spend the Columbus Day weekend with Poppa. They had just converted the propeller flights to jet service from Providence to Washington, and I could be home in an hour. I wasn't much on prop flights, all thanks to those puddle-prop flights our family took going to St. Thomas for the few times we went there. The only way to get to the Virgin Islands back in the day was an eight-hour Pan-Am prop flight from New York into Puerto Rico. Momma hated those flights, too.

"If it weren't for my mother, I wouldn't take this trip," Momma said during every flight.

There were no direct flights to St. Thomas, and I remember the stomach problems brought on by Rolaids and saltine crackers given on the flight. The flights would connect to the island via those puddle-hopper prop Prinair or Caribair planes from the San Juan airport. If you didn't know God, you would find your Creator quickly when landing at the Harry Truman, St. Thomas airport. In the summer of 1959, I took my first island trip to meet Momma's family.

I cried for hours on a Pan Am Trans Atlantic trip with those connecting Puerto Rican flights. Poppa was coming at the end of the summer; he would meet us for vacation. I couldn't stand to be away from Poppa for one moment; I always feared being away from him. Now the memory of island prop flights made me beyond anxious, but I didn't care what it took. I wanted to see Poppa. I knew exactly what Momma meant about going back to visit her home, and we at least agreed on the topic of prop flights going home.

It was great to be home with Poppa for the 1970 Columbus Day Weekend. My heart was always in such a knot about my relationship with Momma that all of it didn't seem to matter anymore. I began to accept that our relationship for what it is, having realized that I only wanted peace. I was making the best of a no-win situation; recapturing moments for any relationship-building future seemed elusive. The weekend was short, and my parents took me to the airport for my flight back to Providence when it was over. Momma lagged back at the departure gate after a kiss and a farewell embrace. Poppa walked me to the boarding gate door.

"Our jet flight service tonight has been changed for the flight bound for Providence. We are now boarding our prop service. Passengers seated in the rear seats please begin boarding now." Looking out the gates window, I could see the plane's propellers twirling. My throat tightened, and my skin-tone changed from light to green. Poppa must've noticed.

"Poppa, I don't want to go," I said, beginning to cry. Poppa looked in my eyes, and held my hand. He spoke prophetically.

"Baby, you can make it alone. Just sit over the wings; the exit door is there and will always be the way of escape." Poppa was right, and I made it back to Providence just fine.

When I got back to school, I couldn't wait for Thanksgiving Break, because I'd see Poppa and Phillip again. It was a very quick Friday night flight, just long enough to have been served a soda and snack. The plane landed at the shuttle gate, and I exited the plane with carry-on luggage in hand, my purse over my shoulder blade, and my portfolio tucked underneath my arm. Home at last, I walked down the gateway into the visitor's receiving area. The first person I saw was Uncle Jack, and Momma was standing by his side. It was a normal thing to see Poppa's right hand man around, so I didn't think it was strange that Poppa wasn't around. It wasn't until I examined their facial expressions that I knew something was wrong. My footsteps toward them halted, and I stood flat-footed before them both.

"Sit down, ma'an," Momma said in a hushed tone. They had planned for Uncle Jack to tell me the news. "Cheryl, Poppa is in the hospital. We didn't want to tell you and upset you at school. He's at the George Washington Hospital Center for tests. We are taking you over to see him, ok?" Their faces were revealing what their hearts were telling them; they didn't need tests to know Poppa's fate. I didn't know what to say. From that moment on, I never spoke a word about Poppa being ill. Ever since I was a toddler, every time Poppa left me, it felt as though he was never coming back. Whenever Poppa traveled, his time away from home would drive me crazy. Poppa was my life coach and support system.

Uncle Jack drove Momma and me to the hospital. Poppa was his usual gregarious self, and quite happy to see me. "Poppa, what's happening?"

"I think I ate too much at an evening business reception and it might have inflamed my gall bladder. I'm having exploratory surgery. Since it's Thanksgiving weekend, they are letting me check out, but I have to be on the operating table Monday morning. I'll be fine," Poppa said.

I did find out that Phillip was on a Greyhound bus traveling home. The trip up from the south took twelve hours overnight, so I would see him in the morning. I was hopeful about Poppa and pleased that Phillip was pressing home to see me. I played off the entire hospital episode saga and focused on expecting Phillip's arrival for the holiday. Wednesday morning, Poppa checked out of the hospital promising doctors he would return Monday morning for his operation. It was great to be at home, and with Phillip, too. Everything was typical for a family Thanksgiving dinner. Poppa sat at the head of the dining table, a little crunched and cramped over it. There was a hollowness in his eyes.

I don't think he knew exactly what his diagnosis would be. I believe he suspected his fate, as he was well aware of his family's health history. I am sure his lurking memory broke thoughts of peace as he remembered his own early college days when his father had taken ill. Pops' living with colon cancer haunted him. I will always remember Pops wearing one of those colon bags which protruded out over his left hip. It peeped through his suit coat for all to see; it was a daily sign that he was wrestling with colon cancer. Cancer hit Pops early, but he lived a full life after having had colon surgery. Poppa knew what I would be facing in my primary college years with a sick father at home since he lived through a similar nightmare.

We got through our family dinner and enjoyed it. I shared my final weekend moments with Phillip and his family; I was back on the airplane to Providence by Sunday evening. I just thought Poppa's hospital situation would blow over and go away; I just had to get myself through the end of the semester. The results came in on Monday evening, and the dorm hall phone rang. I must have been on the floor by myself that evening. The hallway was dim and still.

"Cheryl, the phone is for you. It's your mother," one of my classmates called out. I answered the phone, and I don't remember the opening dialog or our preliminary words.

"Cheryl, the doctors opened your father up. He has an inoperable tumor. He has pancreatic cancer and the tumor cannot be removed. They opened him up and looked in, then closed him back up. He has 10 months to live. Cheryl, Poppa is going to die," Momma said.

I went back home in the morning to be with my family.

There were few words spoken between Poppa and me over the next ten months. God forgive me, I couldn't even say goodbye to him. No one in the family could speak. My only thought was, "Oh God, what am I going to do without Poppa?"

"My little family, my little family, oh Lord," we could hear Poppa whispering as his final months passed. Poppa didn't want his family, his friends, his colleagues, or his co-workers to be informed of his fate. Poppa had finally worked his way to the top of a high-powered Labor Department job. Poppa had a lot resting on his shoulders: board seats, committees, councils, the D.C. government, the D.C. Mayor's office, and his White House appointment to D.C.'s Mayoral Cabinet. He was the next likely choice in succession for the appointed Mayor–Commissioner post. In 1974, the closure of Mayor Walter Washington's appointed tenure was clearly in sight. Having a career plan all the way from college, Poppa didn't see the death's door closing his future view to the beginning of Home Rule, Walter Washington's subsequent elected victory as the Mayor of the District of Columbia, and Marion Barry walking into his dream of becoming the second black Mayor of the District of Columbia. Poppa loved Washington, D.C. and was a real unsung hero in raising the community to a then-greater level never before seen in our nation's capital.

Although a brilliant man, Poppa was vulnerable to the trends and trappings which modeled success. Poppa was a real "cool" smoker, carrying a gold cigarette case and even puffing away with fancy pearled cigarette holders. Granny Sabino had kept him furnished with the best of island smoking gift accessories from Denmark and around the world. Career photos capturing keynote speaking, television tapings, meeting roundtables, business receptions all feature Poppa smoking cigarettes.

Cancer doesn't care about your race.

Poppa's plan was gone now, even though he kept moving along, trying to defy the odds of living over dying. He wanted to purchase a stereo for my dorm room and give me a Christmas gift. We had gone into a stereo store in Chillum, MD, and selected a modest turntable stereo combination. Poppa popped the trunk to put the box in the back of the car. Looking through the rear view mirror, I could see him buckle over, vomiting. He returned to the car with tears in his eyes.

Silent was the night of Christmas 1970. Momma was beyond brave, caring for her ailing husband with no support system at all. Poppa would teach her the basics of household management while we watched him dwindle away. Evenings where Momma and Poppa would slip away for intimacy had turned into nightly meetings in Poppa's office to look at house files. Poppa was keeping everything of importance in The Green Box, and he was turning the keys over to her. Upon returning to college after the winter break, I was speechless through my spring months away from home. I have no idea what my brother was experiencing. We never spoke about what was happening.

Summer was upon us, and Phillip would be home for school summer break. As I was drifting from Poppa's paternal care, I was falling more and more in love with Phillip. We did our best to resume the fun and kindle our lingering love as it had been in high school. Phillip had no idea that he would have to share Poppa's closing moments with us as a family over his summer break. Poppa had become a middle-framed skeleton by summer break. Hospital stays during the spring months were concluding, and his final hospital checkout was at hand. Poppa had been in and out of the hospital since his initial diagnosis, and finally, he'd been sent home to die. Following hospice orders from Poppa's doctors, Momma ordered a hospital bed and had it placed in their bedroom. She was planning to sleep by his side. I will never forget picking Poppa up from his last hospital stay during the midsummer. Phillip had come to visit as usual in the afternoons. His regular "drop over" visits were always strategically scheduled around late afternoons, near Momma's kitchen doorway. Although Mrs. Miller worked evenings and always left dinner on the stove top, Momma's regular island cooking dinner invitations lured him around the house nightly around serving time.

Phillip came to the house to find us gathering, ready to pick Poppa up from the hospital. Phillip drove us to the hospital, drove us back, and decided to help get my father from the car to the bedroom.

Poppa couldn't walk and wouldn't be able to get upstairs without being carried.

"Mr. Holmes, let me help you," Phillip said when he offered Poppa assistance to the house.

Poppa looked at Phillip in the eyes.

"Ok, son, thank you."

Phillip scooped Poppa up like a baby, turned him across his parallel, opened arms, and lifted him from the car. He carried my father up the front entrance stairway, into the house, up the steps of the center hallway staircase to the top landing, down the hallway, and around the corner to the master bedroom. Phillip laid Poppa in the hospital bed, having carried Poppa for the last time through the house he so cherished.

The time had come to inform Poppa's crazy family that Poppa was dying.

"Horace, I think you should call your Mother," Momma told Poppa. By this point, only a handpicked selection of co-workers, fraternity brothers, and cousins were allowed to come by. One of Poppa's favorite cousins, Marlene, was the only member of Poppa's paternal family who was openly welcome by Momma. Momma allowed Marlene to speak with Poppa on the phone. Marlene thought Poppa was ill and recuperating, but not dying. As the moments of Poppa's transition drew closer, Momma ceased all visitations, phone calls and began to insist that Poppa's family should be notified. Against his will, she called Granny Sadie.

It was a steamy Mid-Atlantic Sunday in August 1971 when Momma called for the Holmes tribe. On that Sunday, no High Ball libations were served. Momma had to greet Poppa's family, who had harassed her for over two decades. Their caravan arrival pattern was the same as it had been. Letting Poppa's family into her home was the last thing she wanted to do, and it was the final episode of her personal mixed-nuts soap opera in America. The doorbell rang. Baby Brother and I were in the living room when Momma answered the door. Granny Sadie, Pops, Uncle Landon, Aunt Mary, and Uncle Stanley came through the front door. They were bewildered and had no idea that the situation was so grave. One at a time, they marched upstairs to Poppa's bedside. I remained on the first floor. Pops was the last to visit, toting his Bible in hand. I suppose he was offering Poppa his Last Rites in Christ. I can't imagine what transpired upstairs in such silence, but I knew there was trouble coming. Uncle Stanley seethed in the foyer as though he would implode. He turned red and began blowing up like a balloon when he finally opened his mouth to shout at Momma.

"You kept him from us. You kept him from us."

I am sure Poppa heard it all. He just laid corpse-like in the bed sipping liquids and evaporating from us. Monday morning didn't come fast enough. It was the last Sunday we ever had to worry about Poppa's family coming to visit. It was the last Sunday I saw them all together as a family in my home. It was the last Sunday ever.

OMEGA

I was facing Monday morning once again. It was August 1971, and I had to start thinking about going back to Providence for school. Phillip had taken a job with the Department of Agriculture for the summer, and my precious moments with him were ending. While we enjoyed lunch at the Potomac basin, Momma was busy at home with her morning routine of caring for Poppa. I ignored my guilty feelings about leaving for lunch, and I did that because I was in denial mode. This drama was not happening to me. I did everything I could do to push the Sunday scene out of my mind.

"Love, I have to go. I have to get back home," I told Phillip as our lunch ended.

"Listen, call me if you need anything. I am here. Just take me back to the job, and I'll be praying for you." Phillip sent me home with a kiss, and I dashed to return Phillip back to his office. I hopped on the Rock Creek Parkway speeding back up to the house. I would have never forgiven myself if Poppa had slipped away and I was *limin'* at the Potomac River with my teenage lover. Momma, Chico, and I sat around Poppa. He was lying quietly, sipping liquids, and waiting for his imminent death. The angelic host was gathering. The doorbell rang.

"Ma'an, go open da door," Momma said to me. I ran down and looked through the peephole.

"Momma, it's Aunt Mamie," I shouted.

"My God, what does she want? Hurry, let her in. I have to watch your father." Although Momma didn't know it at the time, the good Lord had sent Aunt Mamie over to be with her. I escorted Aunt Mamie up to the bedroom for Poppa's moments of transition.

"Norma, you have been on my mind for days. I felt we were losing touch. I haven't heard from you in months. I stopped here to see what was happening," Aunt Mamie said. "I had no idea Horace was sick." Poppa's throat began to rattle. It seemed as though the air had grown thick making it harder for us to breathe. Aunt Mamie gently placed her fingertips across Poppa's forehead from temple to temple; her little pinky perched up like she was sipping tea.

"In the name of Jesus, be healed, breathe," she commanded. Now I am here to tell you I have been in church a long time. You name it in the Spirit, I have seen it, from folks barking for deliverance to hysterical laughter overtaking the saints. I have yet to see again what happened at Aunt Mamie's command the day Poppa died. Even her miracle painting couldn't help us, now.

"In the name of Jesus, be healed, breathe."

Poppa's body levitated in the air at every command of authority. Three times, the body levitated up and then flopped back down as if the power of God forced a wind under Poppa's frame and tossed his frail body in the air. Poppa's body plopped up and down like someone shaking out a thick, wet tarp. Poppa was going to die, and the time had arrived for his earthly departure.

"In the name of Jesus, be healed, breathe."

Poppa sat straight up. He opened his eyelids and looked Aunt Mamie squarely in the eyes.

"No. Let me go," Poppa said.

Aunt Mamie removed her hand. Poppa's lifeless body collapsed back down on the bed. All of us sat there stunned.

Uncle Jack made all the funeral arrangements with Momma, and I got to draw a sketch for Poppa's tombstone. Poppa's family was a set of loose cannons loaded with grief, disbelief and anger. They assumed that Momma had kept them from their family hero. That was far from the truth, as Momma was behind the scenes making sure Poppa was being responsible by sharing his condition with his family. Poppa wanted peace while he died, and his family wouldn't have been peaceful. They were volatile and keeping them contained in a separate reception area seemed appropriate after the wake. No doubt, they were offended.

By Friday evening, the viewing and funeral services were over. Held at St. Luke's Episcopal Church, the funeral was uneventful. All of Washington's finest were there from near and far, asking the same questions:

"Why and how could this have happened to a great community leader and activist?"

"So young, oh my goodness, why did this happen to someone so young?"

The burial was held at Lincoln Memorial Parkway Cemetery, one of Washington's most prominent African American cemeteries. At the grave site, the bugle horn cracked the sequential notes of "Taps" followed by the sounds of 21 distinctive gun shots. The sputtering, crisp snaps of aimless gunpowder Pops were fired toward the heavens. The soldiers folded Ol' Glory in unison until it was a triangular shaped pillow, and one of the soldiers placed the folded flag in Momma's lap. Standing amongst only a few graves, Poppa was without peer resting on a hill.

Everyone followed us to the house for the after-service repast. It was pretty uneventful, mixing the joy of seeing old friends with the sorrow of such a tragic loss. By evening, the house was empty. Just as fast as our home filled to the brim with friends, family, and work associates, it emptied out. We never saw most of them again; a beautiful young woman with Poppa's inheritance was too much of a threat in his fast-moving D.C. community. Poppa's friends pretty much all vanished away, especially their wives. The party was over.

I didn't hear from most of Poppa's family for forty years. I would funeralize both my Uncles for their surviving family members, but the large body of Poppa's family never contacted us again. Ask anyone in-the-know about the situation, and they'll say I'm telling the truth. The strife of two decades left us all bitter and raw. Praise God, Momma didn't have to deal with Sadie ever again.

Phillip's mother died the year after Poppa, and his dad had passed away when Phillip was young. Momma was left to seeing Chico, Phillip and me through young adulthood. We only had each other by that point, or at least Momma and Chico had each other. I pretty much remained outside of everything. I transferred from Providence to complete my college years at the Maryland Institute College of Art in Baltimore moving closer home to be with Momma. Phillip became disenchanted with school down south and enrolled in American University's business school. We got engaged.

Momma depended on my weekend visits to get to the grocery store and Poppa's grave site. For years, Momma and I would attend to Poppa's resting place on Sundays. Though quite a long trip from home across town, it was the least I could do after all I had put her through as a child.

Momma sold Poppa's long, green, gangster-lean 1970 Cadillac El Dorado because it was too big for her drive. Instead she purchased a small compact car. Poor thing, Momma did her best to drive to work, although she did so like a little ol' woman. Poppa's mark of excellence, the revered Washington, D.C. low tag license plate number "168" was reassigned to an unknown D.C. government official.

"Momma, why don't you go home to the islands? Get away from Washington, we'll be fine," I told her some years after Poppa passed. Although Chico was in high school, Phillip and I promised Momma we would see to his needs. She took our advice and a vacation. Providence would greet her at the Dulles International Airport on her way to St. Thomas, and she would find John, who was newly-divorced. He had been a high school classmate of Momma's. They found each other again along the shores of Paradise with "Yellow Bird" and "Hot, Hot, Hot" filling their hearts. It was their life's bond together. They eventually married and lived peacefully enjoying their island culture—food, dancing, island gossipin', limin', and traveling. John was just what Momma needed; a man from her culture.

Momma and I found peace, but the time for pouring glue upon our relationship had passed. At the very least, she knew she could depend on me to get things done even with Poppa gone. Without my knowing it, she put my name on things of importance, such as the ownership of Poppa's burial plot. Phillip and I decided to get married the last year of college. I married a beautiful man who could make more money than my Poppa; I followed Momma's advice. I think Poppa even could see we had fallen in love.

Father Walker became Bishop John Thomas Walker, the first African-American Bishop of the Episcopal Diocese of Washington. He kept his promise to me, and married me and Phillip at the National Cathedral. His Bishop's wedding blessing has kept us together over the years. He knotted his Bishop's stole around our locked hands, sealing our vows through so many ups and downs. Uncle Jack stood in for Poppa and gave me away during the ceremony. Of course, the best wedding photographer couldn't air brush out the somber look upon all of our faces. Poppa wasn't there, and each picture captured our loss.

Phillip finished business school with an MBA in hand, and we adventured off to New York's tri-state gateway. His family received me as their own, since I had no paternal family relationships and my maternal family was too far away. More than that, with Momma, John and Baby Brother in a world of their own, I bonded with the Miller family.

I grafted into the Miller's church world and their church legacy, which consisted of several generations of African Methodist Episcopal clergy. I learned all about the black church as I embraced their Christian heritage. I became dedicated to the African-American church. I couldn't deny Sadie and her people were church builders; it was in my spiritual legacy whether I liked it or not.

I concentrated on my design career, which flourished in New York City. I opened a corporate communications design firm and furthered my design education by attending graduate school at Pratt Institute. I enjoyed a fair amount of notoriety, traveling, speaking, winning awards, writing trade articles, and servicing national clients. I was eventually labeled as being one of the top Black Designers in America. I took Booker T. Washington's strategy for young Negro men, "Be better than the best white boy," to heart. I did the absolute best I could to embrace elite, white male dominated professions, with no mentors, as a black woman.

I have even received one of Dorothy Height's revered "Crystal Staircase" Awards. Dorothy Height, a longtime civil rights activist, president emeritus of the National Council of Negro Women and one of the Godmothers of the women's movement honored African-American women yearly with her prestigious award for their accomplishments.

It was Poppa teaching me of Alice Walker's womanist theology and this black woman's overachiever self-esteem which sent me soaring for greater heights, where even no man has ever even gone. The frontier took me deep into Cathy Thompson's reflective book titled *Biracial Women in Therapy: Between the Rock of Gender and the Hard Place of Race* which spoke to my life's squeeze. Being multi-racial, I have lived in the place where race and gender nearly squeezes the life out of you.

Barack Obama describes a scenario similar to my immediate family's in his memoir *Dreams From My Father.* While working as a young organizer in Chicago, he relates to Mary, a co-worker. Mary, a white woman with biracial daughters, had become active and embedded in the urban plight of South Chicago. He understood her "no turning back after marrying a black man situation," and he understood what it meant to be left with biracial children. Obama's anecdote floods a halogen light on my mother's situation at the time.

"Somehow she had met a black man...they dated secretly...were married...then the man left...and Mary found herself beached in a world she knew little of, without anything but the house and two manila hued daughters, unable to return to the world she had known."

Obama saw his mother's situation in Mary. Although death removed Momma's black man from view, I see my situation in Obama's situation. I see my situation in Mary's situation, too. Poppa died and left Momma with mulatto, mixed race children in his Negro world. Her return to the shores of Paradise was not an option.

Obama relates to Mary as I relate to Obama's own reflections of being abandoned by his African father, needing a race because he is half African and half white American by his mother. He describes the cavity between the rock and the hard place as being *"occupied in the place where their dreams had been."* In that broad stroke where it all collapses down, my brother and I were left half African-American and half Philippine-American with a culturally Danish West Indian mother embedded in our father's Negro world. Momma was just left alone; Horace Jr. and I became lost children within the framework of our family structure. Poppa always had a master plan, but didn't plan on dying and leaving Marion Barry to walk into our once dream, now nightmare.

Momma had money in the bank to fulfill the dreams of her children. Although she never made chocolate chip cookies for me as she did my brother, she sure sent us both a check for $10,000.00 in a brown envelope on a single occasion.

"Ma'an, here take it while I am alive. It might be 'tru by da time I'm dead 'n gone. Here, take da cash now. Enjoy."

Momma packed up all of her life's files with Poppa and stuffed them into The Green Box. For many years, that box would remain buried in the basement of Momma and Poppa's home; the home that John moved into as his own. Momma was an extremely blessed woman in spite of all that transpired in her early years in America. Over and against illnesses, she was continually healed and cured from attacking diseases. The Lord sent a brand new husband to take her into her future, and her kids flourished. I couldn't imagine how, but I knew my mother's words would haunt me the rest of my life.

Ma'an yah gonna miss me. Yah dunt mis da wadder till the well run dry.

Karma, godly revenge, you reap what you sow...who is to know how destiny manifests. In Momma's case, words always came to pass. I left home to face my adult future, not realizing that Momma's words would meet me again at my middle passageway.

Momma hungered to locate the father who had abandoned her. I learned to live without Poppa.

My father desired to be the Mayor of Washington D.C. His career strategy ended with his untimely death in 1971. What would I do without Poppa? Oh My God, what would Momma do without Poppa?

PART II

"When my father and my mother forsake me,

then the LORD will take me up."

–Psalms 27:10

THE WAR INJURY

I was totally estranged from my paternal family for nearly forty years. And while I love Momma's island family, distance and cultural differences have often made it difficult for us to understand each other. There was little, if anything, they could do to support me during the familial struggles of my childhood. The funny thing about the war that destroyed my relationship with my paternal family is, that in the end, everyone lost.

It's far too late in the season of my life to recover most of my family, as most are dead. Over the course of my life, I've learned two important lessons: you can't pick the family you're born into, and no one can replace that family. I apply those harsh-to-learn lessons toward my own family because I won't allow history to repeat itself.

Time did not heal my physical or emotional war injuries. My tooth is still chipped, and I'll always carry some level of guilt for never bonding with Momma, even if we stopped fighting after Poppa's death. Both Sadie's war with Momma and my war with Momma ended on the hill where we buried my father, but the end of that war gave way to a new one for me: the war within.

In every battle of the war within, I am surrounded, outnumbered, ambushed, and outgunned. I had but one "enemy" in my war with Momma. In my war within, I face a full axis comprised of my enemies Shame, Anger, Guilt, Regret, and the enemies I fear most, Ostracism, Stigmatism and Being an Enigma. My war with Momma threatened to tear our immediate family apart, but my war within has threatened to tear my soul apart, and leave a gaping, terrible, ravenous black hole in its place.

The most important thing to know about my darkest inner space is that I can't even really explain it, its impacts on my life, or the shapes that it takes from season to season. Besides Phillip, only one person in my entire life has ever noticed or suggested that, sometimes, I hurt beyond comprehension. She was a fan of my ministry.

"Reverend Miller, you are a godly woman, but you know, there is something wrong," she said to me after a Sunday sermon. The result was that I drew my distance from her convinced that she could somehow perceive that unidentifiable "something" within me. I didn't want her to "see" my anomaly before I could figure it out myself. I didn't want to reveal the existence of my black hole to anyone.

However, my abyss, which seeks to gorge itself on the light of my being, has never prevented me from succeeding in life. The Grace of God has kept me from succumbing to the fury of this raging, inner breach by blessing me with knowledge and God's wisdom. More than that, I can arm others for their wars within, especially those closest to me.

As I grew into middle-age, I would engage in a decisive battle for my soul. Of all things, it was buried truths of The Green Box, the love of God and the love of my real family that finally waked me from my tragic mulatto nightmare.

C.D. Holmes-Miller along the journey of self discovery.

An Odyssey Begins 1992

My odyssey toward truth began in 1992, the year I entered seminary. I was given an assignment to create a family tree of intergenerational social origins.

"Oh, my family on-up from slavery, that's a good one," I grumbled to myself. The only one who could help me was our family's archivist, Aunt Mary. In 1992, she was elderly, but she still remembered every bit of the war between my family and Sadie's. The minute I called her, I became the heir apparent to Aunt Mary's legacy of being my paternal family's archivist. I was just trying to fulfill and complete a seminary class project not find out anything about my race, family or otherwise. Aunt Mary collected family obituaries; she just loved going to family funerals. Organizing the funeral service bulletins and keeping them all in order was her hobby. Everyone's stories were on the back of the bulletins. All I needed to do was seam together the obituary stories, and I would learn all about my family.

Although they had been hurtful folks, I wanted to focus on my paternal family's tree. There were just too many mixed-raced issues for us to live peacefully as a family. Granny Sadie's folks were both Holiness and Baptist church folks, ministers or church planters. I figured my propensity for ministry had come from her side of the family — "Yah faddah's people, 'dem," as Momma would say. While I was not fond of them, whether I liked it or not, they were family.

"Aunt Mary, this is Cheryl," I said to Aunt Mary when I called her for the obituaries.

"Hey, Lady," Aunt Mary answered, her voice raspy from a late-night awakening.

"Aunt Mary, can you send me your obituary collection? I have a project for school. I have to prepare a family tree."

"Cheryl, yes, of course. I'll forward them right away, but," Aunt Mary's usual jovial tone became slightly more serious, "send them back."

"I will. Now, tell me a joke."

A stuffed brown envelope arrived in the mail a few weeks later, and it was filled with treasured obituaries, countless church bulletins, and letters. I found stories of my family through short summaries of their lives, which included the church positions that they served in. There was also a handwritten letter explaining Mary's life with Uncle Landon, and a mysterious ten page document from a cousin I didn't know. This cousin had gone to the National Archives and mapped out our paternal family. Marlene had that document, knew of my school project, and sent it to Aunt Mary. Aunt Mary sent it to me with the obituaries. The document recorded locator file numbers for each census record, and additional microfiche details were noted on each page.

Cousin Marlene carefully embellished the pages exhaustively with red footnotes and explanations for each family member mentioned in the narrative. She filled the front page with contact information should I need to reach her. I didn't know the author of the original document as a family member, but I kept it among my files for my project. Pops' race was recorded as "MU," I call it the "M Factor." This document would become my *Red Letter Bible*.

I put the document in an envelope with all of my other research notes for the class. I placed it in a cardboard box, and put the box on the top shelf of my closet. It would stay there for 16 years because I didn't need it for my class project. As I began to organize all of the bulletins, I noticed they all had something special in common. One minister, Bishop Kent T. Holmes, had funeralized everyone in my family. His name, the name of the church, address and phone number were listed on the backs and fronts of all of the folded bulletins. Each bulletin cover had a picture of my respective family member and their obituary information. I needed Bishop Holmes to sign off on the information, so I called him at 10:30 p.m. that night.

"Good evening, Northeast Church of the Holy Trinity Apostolic Faith. May I help you," a church secretary answered in surprise.

"Oh Lawdy, it was a working number," I choked. "Hello, my name is Cheryl Holmes-Miller. Is Bishop Holmes available?"

"Oh yes, he is in a church meeting. I will bring him to the phone."

"No, please...if he is in a church meeting, please don't disturb him."

"H'llo," a man's voice boomed. I knew it was the bishop.

"Bishop, this is Cheryl Holmes-Miller, Sadie's granddaughter. I am in seminary, and I have this project to make a family tree. I have family obituaries before me, and you seemed to have buried most of our family over the years. Can you tell me about my family?"

"Oh yes, I know you. Hmn, seminary, huh?" Bishop Holmes chuckled. "Well, God bless."

"Bishop, are you still active in the ministry?"

"Active at 89," Bishop Holmes paused. "You know, Granny's own grandfather was white."

I was stunned at first, as Sadie was very dark brown like a Hershey's Kiss, albeit a bitter one. Yes, Sadie's grandfather was white, and her grandmother Margaret was a black woman. I had most definitely been fooled.

"Robert, your great-grandfather, was black and white. Sadie and I were first cousins. My father, Gordon Holmes, and Sadie's mother, Alberta were brothers and sister," revealed Bishop Holmes. Future research confirmed his every word to be true, especially regarding my great-grandparents Robert and Alberta Acty from Madison County, Virginia. Robert and his wife Alberta were marked "MU" all over the census records. Great-Grandpa Robert was marked "mulatto" in 1880 when he was nine years old living with his mother Margaret; she was black.

Then he was marked black in 1900 and 1910. He was marked in 1920 as a "mulatto." In my great-grandfather's day, the Madison County, Virginia town clerk was the census enumerator. He obviously couldn't figure out exactly how to identify great-grandpa Robert according to changing enumeration guidelines every ten years.

Finishing the project led to completing my degree program at Union Theological Seminary. I thought nothing more of my project, or of my crazy, dead, disenfranchised paternal family. I had previously graduated with an MS in Communications Design from Pratt Institute, managed my New York City design business, was ordained to the Gospel Ministry, and started my own church. I lived on just fine without so much of a memory of Poppa's people.

Poppa's maternal family-the Acty's, my African-American family, has spiritua origins in establishing churches. My black paternal grandmother, Sadie, rejected my mother as a marital choice for her favored son, my father. The mixed race drama disenfranchised our family for a lifetime.

An Odyssey Continues 2000

When Momma died in June 2000, The D.C. Coroner marked Momma's race on her death certificate as being "black." That's not what her birth certificate noted, but that's the way her story ended.

Momma kept on ticking in spite of two rounds of cancer, renal disease, and renal heart failure. She called it her "Organ Recital," one organ failing after another. In 1949, Momma's brother Emilio had died of kidney failure at age 28. Kidney disease ran in the family, and in Emilio's era, there was no treatment for it. Momma always believed that if she could find her Filipino father, she would learn more about her own health history.

In old age, Momma would often ask me to help her find her father. It always bothered her that her Filipino father had abandoned her at such an early age because she'd always desired a father-daughter relationship. She hung onto the thought of him in her life, although she only knew him from shared scrapbook pictures. Sinforoso made us Filipinos, but at the same time, he didn't exist to us.

Each member of my maternal family had tried, in their own way, to solve the mystery of our Asian grandfather's whereabouts. Momma searched for him and her possible "other" family her entire life, yet never found them either. She would comb the White Pages for her missing father every time we traveled to a new city, especially New York City, where she would care for Granny Sabino's sister, Aunt Blanche. My God, I feel so guilty that I never obliged her requests to help her find my grandfather. I would usually tease her a little and brush her request off.

"Momma, just how am I going to find a turn of the century Asian man who doesn't want to be found?" I would shrug, too. "Momma, you are watching too much Ricki Lake in the afternoon."

I had all sorts of excuses for avoiding my long-lost grandfather. The best excuse was that I would find him and he would probably be dead. I ignored her, and I developed a habit of smiling, listening, and nodding my head in agreement as though I was serious about following up on her request.

"Why don't you ask my brother for all of these things, since you both had it that way with each other," I grumbled to myself. The only request I honored from Momma was her request that I preside over her funeral service. It was the least I could do to be a *good island daughtah.* Momma had two services: one in D.C. and one in St. Thomas.

Phillip and I went to D.C. after the funeral to collect Momma's things from the home she and John lived in, the home that John would live in until his own death. It was the 4th of July weekend. With our car packed to the brim, Phillip went to the mail box to pick up the mail before getting on the road.

"Cheryl, I think you need to see this," Phillip said as he read a letter he'd just opened.

"What's up with that mystery letter in your hand," I replied. He gave me the letter, and took a break from packing.

The letter read:

Elder, please give this letter and this Ancestry.com post to Pastor when you think she is ready to read it. Margaret

I ran to the computer to reply. The next leg of my odyssey had begun, and the path for the journey had been paved long before I walked it. Momma, along with my church congregation and family, attended my 25th wedding anniversary service. While she was there, Momma met Margaret, a research librarian and former member of my church. Momma discovered Margaret was a researcher, and I could just hear her whispering into Margaret's ear,

"Can you help me find my father?"

I suppose Margaret took Momma's request to heart. The results were in; she had discovered another family online searching for Sinforoso Jose Sabino on Ancestry.com. She copied the post and sent it to me. As it turns out, Sinforoso had abandoned another family. Margaret had sent the letter to Phillip, probably under the belief that I would not be ready for such a discovery. Phillip had been tasked with sharing the letter with me when it was appropriate, and he'd decided to share it with me before even he read it.

The Ancestry.com post scrolled before my eyes:

I am trying to help my mother find information about her father, my grandfather. His name was Sinforoso Jose Sabino...

Lawdy, did I know that cry in the wilderness. The post was written by a woman named Susan, and she was my newfound cousin. I wrote and e-mailed her as soon as I could. She replied in an instant. We soon spoke on the phone, and there are few words to explain the supernatural power of our connection. After all, we could find common ground in our grandfather, who had emotionally marred our mothers with his abandonment. Thirty days to Momma's passing, I found both Sinforoso and Momma's half-sister. Sinforoso, Momma, Poppa, Granny Sabino, Granny Sadie, the Heavenly Host, and the Lord God Almighty all worked together to pour down their truths and lead me again to The Green Box, which might as well have been Heaven's cabinet cascading files to me. God's timing is simply impeccable.

"Call my mom, and I will contact you when I get settled in my new home," Susan told me over the phone. Susan was packing up for a road trip, like me, but she was moving to the West Coast from Boston. I spoke to her mother, my new Aunt Tommy, who confirmed that her family and our "Sinforosos" were the same. By the time I finally got to Washington for the 4th of July, Aunt Tommy and I were already engaging photo exchanges through e-mail. Aunt Tommy began to tell me all about her siblings and her mother.

"It seems my father also left my mother as he did your grandmother. I was one of four children, and he left us when my youngest brother was a little over a year old. I was 10, and we never heard from him again. I was named after his mother, and my sister is named after his sister. My oldest brother is deceased. He was a twin, and his twin only lived a few months. They were born in 1922," Aunt Tommy said.

My family's mystery was solved in that one email and its attachments. He had used the same given names from our family to name the children of their family. Aunt Tommy's brother had been born between my Uncle Emilio in 1921 and 1923, when my mother was born. Sinforoso sired children with two women of nearly the same racial composition. As an Asian man in America's turn of the century naval ports, mixed women were his only option for relationships. My grandmother was black and Irish; the Danish called her "mixed." And Tommy's mother was an unknown admixture of Caucasian. The two wives looked alike, right down their bitter, lovelorn expressions. Still hidden from us was Sinforoso's original Filipino family.

I spent the entire summer mourning my mother's death by finding all of Sinforoso's vital records. Aunt Tommy wanted to come to New York and meet me. As providence would have it, we met for lunch on my mother's birthday at Grand Central Station's Grand

Hyatt Restaurant. Aunt Tommy's niece, Louisa, was with her. They were on time, and I was fashionably late. They weren't hard to spot within the usual sea of travelers in Grand Central. Aunt Tommy looked like my mother, and Louisa, my new first cousin, was white. I put that observation in the back of my mind for the moment as I walked toward them.

"Are you looking for your niece," I asked Aunt Tommy. We embraced, and she looked at me trying to see the Sinforoso in me. She pinched me on the cheek.

"You are so pretty," Aunt Tommy squealed. "You're short. I thought you would be taller."

"How could I be? Sinforoso was short." We chuckled and agreed that, although we were mixed, we were Filipinas. In the Philippines, we would be regarded as "mestiza/os" or "FilAms" or "Filipino Amerasians." Over lunch, I took a deep breath, and then let her know that her new family was West Indian and culturally black Afro-Caribbean. We knew that Sinforoso made us Filipinas racially, but in the islands, we had been classified as Negroes since the transitional sale of the Danish West Indies to America. I viewed all of her family pictures; her entire family was white. We are simply Asian Island Creole folks of sorts, just a Virgin Island 'ting ma'an.

"Reverend Miller, I only wanted to know where he had gone when he left us. I never imagined I would discover where he had come from," Aunt Tommy said, her eyes revealing the desires of her heart. "You are so good at this. Please help me find where he went from our family."

Auntie was asking me to do what I could never do for Momma. I left lunch and caught the train back to New England, my mind moving faster than the train itself. From the fall of 2000 to the winter of 2000, I followed Sinforoso's trail. In the winter of 2000, I discovered Sinforoso's death certificate. Sinforoso died in 1973 while living in Hobe Sound, Martin County, Florida. He was Catholic by religion, but certainly not by character. I called Catholic churches in Martin County until I found the church that funeralized Sinforoso, and they gave me the funeral director's name. I called the funeral home which received his body.

"Reverend Miller, that was a long time ago, but we did indeed funeralize your grandfather. His records and obituary would be on microfilm. If you can give me a few days, I will look through the films and read the obituary for you," the funeral director told me when I asked about Sinforoso's funeral. I was anxious for the promised return call, and, several days after I'd made contact with him, the funeral director called back.

"Oh yes, I remember this family quite well. The obituary lists Sinforoso's stepson, who paid for the funeral. Here is the information, maybe you can find the stepson and get more information."

With a single Google search, I found Sinforoso's stepson. He was an acclaimed journalist who was referenced all over the Internet.

Sinforoso's stepson was the first person I'd spoken to in my journey that knew my grandfather as an adult. When I contacted him, he cringed at telling me anything about my grandfather, as the name sickened him. He shared an incredible story of how Sinforoso had ruined his home and married his mother in 1968, the same year that Granny Sabino finally divorced Sinforoso. They ended up living in Florida where he died, was cremated, and tossed to the wind.

The End.

I was excited to introduce my new Aunt Tommy to my island uncle; Momma's last surviving sibling. As I hear it, she enjoyed the trip. I put all of my emails, notes, records, pictures, and everything related to this portion of my journey into the box where I placed my family discoveries from 1992.

Momma chose her racial box as "black" because she wanted to. Meeting my new aunt and her family made me think about Momma's death certificate; Momma's half-sister wasn't black, but Momma declared herself black.

So what did that make me?

Destiny would bring closure to a lifetime of war abandonment disillusionment issues as I met my mother's half sister after her death in 2000. I was united with my Philippine American family and learned the whereabouts of our collective family's missing Filipino father, grandfather. We had the same mystery in common.

THE GREEN BOX
2008

In June of 2008, right after Barack Obama won the Democratic nomination for the 56th Presidential Race, I began to feel the verve of life leaving my heart, body and soul. My black hole had finally hollowed me from the inside out. I can't say what plunged me into that despair; I can only point a very stern-minded finger at certain aspects of the black church culture and some of the people I encountered in it.

The challenges I faced as a female minister had begun to undo the personal sense of empowerment I had been raised with. Animosity for women ministers serving in the church made church life adversarial against my emotional, spiritual and physical safety. I have supported and ministered so many others up the ladder of life that I began slipping spiritually myself.

From the beginning moments of accepting Christ into my life, I have tried to walk Christ's path. Never wavering to the left or to the right, I felt I had to "walk the talk" to succeed in my vocation of the Gospel Ministry, to remain blessed in my secular corporate design career, and to be earnest in all of my relationships. I have received my just share of awards, certificates, honors and kudos articles. I have enough degrees and honorary degrees to paper a wall. I have made so many personal sacrifices and godly choices in the surrendering of plans, purposes, people, places and pleasures over to God's Ultimate Will that I was confident that my good work had surely earned me a place in Heaven. I was at complete peace and without regret, ready to see Jesus face-to-face. I felt like my life was over and I had fulfilled my mission in life. I resigned from my ten year pastorate in order to rest.

I remember the crisp, cool wind blowing through my bedroom window one early summer evening in 2008. New England summers are brisk and gentle, never hot or very humid like my hometown. In a quiet moment before slumber whisked me to the angels, I said goodnight to Phillip in an unusual way.

"Phillip, listen," I paused, and then sighed. "Phillip, if I should die before I wake, please know that I love you, and thank you for giving me the love of a lifetime. Thank you for sharing your life with me, Phillip. I feel like I am going to die. I feel like my life is closing out. It feels like God is preparing me to die and giving me a few moments to clean up matters. I don't want to die, but I sense my work's completion."

"Cheryl, why do you feel like you are going to die," Phillip asked me. "Cheryl, you aren't going anywhere. We have these children to raise. You have me. Why would you say this, Cheryl?"

I didn't die that night. I awakened in the morning, and continued my conversation with Phillip. The silence of the rural, beautiful area we lived in made the dawn seem still. In those quiet moments before speaking, I couldn't believe what I was thinking.

"I've done all I can do as a black woman. There is no more road left for me to walk upon. There are no more first mountains to climb. I am getting older, and there is no more to accomplish. There are no more doors to open, no more points to prove. I don't feel like I've been serving the people that God wants me to serve. I am not able to travel this course any further," I said.

Phillip listened, went across the kitchen for a cup of coffee, and touched my shoulder upon returning to our table. He brought back the local paper and pointed to the front cover. Jesse Jackson and two of the community's black pastors had been photographed at a downtown church, standing together in the iconic Civil Rights "We Will Overcome" criss-cross arm lock. They were celebrating Barack Obama's victory in unity.

"Cheryl, take a real good look at yourself, baby. Do you think you can really stand with these men and represent the black community as a black pastor? This is not about whether you can do the job or not, but stand back and look at that picture," Phillip said. "What do you see?"

Not black enough to be black, white enough to be white, or Asian enough to be Asian, Phillip was highlighting my conundrum. In a broad stroke, black folks couldn't see me as their own, so black church leaders couldn't see me with their voice. No matter how loud I screamed I was a black woman, folks not accustomed to the presence of mixed-race individuals in America would never see me as a black woman. With nothing but time on my hands, Chico and I resolved to finish cleaning out our Washington, D.C. childhood home. For years, we'd owned the home, though we'd avoided doing anything with it because it was too painful for us to return there.

We could never make a decision about what to do with the old home, and we didn't often consider how to settle the estate between ourselves. With our parents and John now deceased, we just couldn't face the inevitable task of clearing the home and possibly putting it up for sale. Washington D. C. was changing, and a new president would change the climate of my hometown for sure. Although I live in New England now, Washington is still home in my heart because it was Poppa's home. Clearing out my parents' home was a symbolic "pulling of the root," which is to say that I wasn't merely moving away, I was leaving my father's hometown for good. My only remaining entitlement to D.C. is my eternal resting place at Lincoln Cemetery where I will lie in peace next to my father.

"Whatever you do, don't sell the house, Norma. It's what you have, you and the kids. You'll always have a home," Poppa told Momma a short time before his death. As a family, we'd obeyed him. Year after year, we just kept looking at a decision we couldn't make. The time had come for us to move past our father's dying wish. Before cleaning the old home out, I took a plunge and signed my half of my parent's house over to my brother, cashing in and opting out. He would stay, and I would go.

"Chico, what do you want to do," I asked my brother.

"I don't know, what do you want to do," Chico replied. "Maybe we should sell it and split the cash."

We shopped around for the best mortgage rates. Chico called a local mortgage company to see how much it would cost to repair the house, fix the roof, or do a mutual buy out between us. The mortgage officer handling the deal couldn't have known that the female mortgage officer on the opposite of his cubicle was kin to the man he was speaking to. Hearing her co-worker repeat my brother's name while on the phone, she motioned to him with excitement.

"That's my cousin. That's my cousin."

Somewhat protective of the sales potential, the co-worker ignored her. Indeed, it was my father's first cousin's daughter, Lisa, and her grandmother Nannie was Sadie's sister- in-law. Nannie had been married to Granny Sadie's brother. Poppa's Aunt Nannie was Lisa's grandmother. I always wondered what happened to Aunt Nannie because she was Poppa's favorite aunt, and Poppa was her favorite nephew. Unfortunately, Aunt Nannie passed away by 2008. Lisa inherited Aunt Nannie's personal bible and a basket of legacy family photos. Tucked between the bible pages was a clipping of my *Washington Post* wedding announcement. It was creased in a seam and had become a part of Nannie's prayer list. If your name was written on a note and tucked in between the pages of Aunt Nannie's bible, she was praying for you. When Lisa inherited the bible, she inherited Aunt Nannie's practice of praying for those in it. When Chico told me he'd spoken to Lisa, I knew that God was guiding me again.

I began taking summer weekend trips for the task of cleaning, closing and sorting out Momma's things. I met Lisa during one of these trips to D.C. and spent the afternoon with her. Taking a deep breath, I began to build a bridge back to my father's maternal family via Lisa. It was unbelievable how much she looked like Sadie, Dear Lord.

We sat over family pictures for hours, examining photos of family members I hadn't been allowed to have a relationship with. From a child's viewpoint, I had come to despise my father's family because of their part in our family drama. As children, we paid a dear price for everyone's inability to accept one another. I had missed a lifetime without knowing my family, and now all I had was Lisa, and she re-introduced me to my long-lost family via old "black in the day" Kodak Moments. Lisa was too young to identify some of the older faces in the pictures. To my surprise, I could identify some of the faces in her ancient collection. For example, Granny Sadie's stern, holier-than-thou look is unforgettable.

The time came for sharing and reflection. I tried to explain how we had been cut off from the family. It was difficult to explain to Lisa and have her understand the devastation of what had happened to us. As our "getting to know me" session was ending, my hand reached for a picture of a woman lying in a coffin.

Black folks love taking funeral pictures.

"Who is this?" I asked.

"Cheryl, I don't know," she replied. I stared at the picture and turned it over, looking for any identifying mark or note. I kept staring at the face in the coffin, and eventually realized I was looking at my Aunt Thelma, Poppa's sister.

"Lawdy. Aunt Thelma," I blurted. I never knew when, where, or how my Aunt Thelma had died. You can't imagine how I felt, attending my aunt's funeral via Lisa's legacy photo basket. I started crying and couldn't stop, reliving the funeral as if I had actually been there. The last photo I picked up ended our meet and greet time together. Aunt Nannie had a beautiful high school photo portrait of my father as a young teen, and I'd never seen the picture before. His bright green eyes seemed to be smiling and watching over me as I met and mourned my family all at the same time. Countless photos of people I had never known wanted me to finally meet them. I met my family and grieved the loss of each one as I sorted through the woven basket of photos that afternoon.

Weekend trips to size up our estate situation were over by the summer's end. Chico was with me for my last trip. The house itself was an E-bay smorgasbord. In fact, every time I visited the house, it was like my parents were still mulling around there. We combed through layers of family memorabilia. Momma had just rolled, tucked and hid her trinkets all over the house. Her ephemera, secret fractals, photos and especially anything she had of Poppa's was all hidden away. Chico and I had to open every book, leaf through every page, unroll every piece of quilting cloth and remnant scrap. Momma saved and hid everything as if she was preparing for a hurricane that never came; it was the island way.

I knew this particular weekend trip would be the most difficult.

"I've started sorting things out, let's go to the basement," Chico said while we were cleaning together. As it often occurs in life, I didn't think that my life was going to change the way it did when I unlocked and opened the basement door. I didn't think that answers to family secrets and an understanding of my own past were in the basement of the home that I grew up in, the home that my father died in. The journey of the Holmes children was about to reach its apex, and we couldn't guess, at the time, that our paths would lead us to the same place at the same time—the place it all started for us.

We descended down the red marble linoleum stairs into the basement. Redskins team posters, NFL flags and island paintings covered the wall of the basement. The basement was in the same state I remembered it being in when Momma was still alive. Scenes from my childhood replayed in my mind.

"Cheryl, I found Momma's 'green box'. It's right where she left it," Chico said, shaking his head. "I really don't want to open it. I really don't, but we have to."

We had forgotten the file cabinet was even in the house. In order to transact any business with the house, we had to open The Green Box, and we did so with a rusty-crowbar that was in the basement. We took seats side-by side on Poppa's favorite 1960s black art deco sofa. The files were well-organized, and there were so many of them. Mercy, the first folder that my hand happened to touch was my father's will which hadn't been opened since 1971. When we opened the top flap, three cascading photos of Momma, Chico, Phillip, and me fell out of the fold and dropped into my lap. In the pictures, we were standing on Poppa's three day old grave hilltop with our wobbly feet balancing amidst the funeral flowers and bouquets. Uncle Jack was taking the pictures that day. Each picture captured the drama we were facing nearly forty years ago. I stared into the snap shot of Momma's face. She was holding a tattered, tear-soaked tissue to her nose. As we looked at the photos, Chico became sad. It was a back to the future moment.

"Ma'an, ya lookin' a little green around the gills," as Momma might have said to her baby boy.

"God looked out for us." I said to him. "Let's go to Crisfield's for crab cakes."

Truth had been chasing me down, and, now that it'd caught me, it knocked me down to a fetal position of prayer. When we returned to The Green Box, the next thing I found was our parent's marriage license application. Momma was marked as "colored." After Poppa died, Momma hid their wedding photo album in The Green Box.

"Have a look at their marriage license," I said to Chico. He peered at the revealing information, and I just stared at Momma's race, marked "colored," on the document. Momma had to mark herself as colored woman in order to marry a black man in America. Momma entered into the system at that point. I can only imagine their conversations about getting married. They were sandwiched between and around the southern and Mid-Atlantic anti-miscegenation law-abiding states, yet, I remembered Poppa's stories about his courtship of my mother. They loved each other despite the law.

My mind began to wonder to the point that I had an out-of-body experience. I was no longer in the basement with my brother. I drifted into a daydream where I was a little girl again swinging on my father's knee. Rocking back and forth, he began to tell me the story of how he and Momma met, hugging me while we watched television in our 1957 living room. As he told me the story, I went deeper into my waking dream, imagining my father, his friends, and Norma Sabino on the campus of Howard University in 1947.

"From afar, Cheryl, we could see those pristine-capped nurses from Freedmen's Hospital. The nurses were all huddled together, just loving their new uniforms. They looked really good in them, too. My friends and I approached them, and they got prettier and prettier the closer we came to them," Poppa said. He smiled away while telling me the story, and Nat King Cole was performing "*I Love You For Sentimental Reasons*" on the television.

"When we got really close to the huddle, I noticed a woman, so unique and gorgeous. That was your Momma. Cheryl, your

Momma was so pretty." Poppa smoked one of those nasty Kent cigarettes and blew smoke rings all over the living room.

"I advanced toward your Momma; I wanted to meet her. Eventually, I asked her to Howard's 1948 homecoming dance. I was so happy that she agreed. We fell in love, pun'kin. In 1949, when we were graduating, I asked her what her plans were and she told me that she was returning to the islands. I was supposed to marry someone else, but when I met your mother, I knew that she was the one for me. I couldn't have her leave me and go back to her home, so I asked her to marry me." I could hear Nat's smooth melody, "*...I Love You For Sentimental Reasons...*" entwining with my Poppa's love story.

In the basement, tears streamed down my face and nudged me out of my daydream. My focus remained on Momma's race—Dear God, what was Momma's race, really?

We discovered their black and white wedding photo album wrapped up in plastic. I flipped through the photo album, and I found myself envisioning the wedding as if I had an actual memory of it. I broke down into tears and returned the wedding album to The Green Box.

Momma's scrapbook was fascinating, if only because she'd started it from the day she arrived in the States. I discovered Momma's college yearbook which contained photos of my father and her at some of the many black tie events they attended together. There were even newspaper clippings of their cameo appearances about town making guest appearances at a variety of high-brow Negro social events. Her black tie gloves and evening purses, among the pile of memorabilia, smelled like Shalimar. Shalimar was Momma's favorite perfume. I learned all about black tie events, about jewelry and perfume by watching her get dressed to accompany Poppa about town. If she had only explained her culture to me, I would have appreciated her culture so much more. I would have loved her more.

It was my mother's birth certificate which thrust me into one of the most compelling segments of my journey and made me question my own identity. By examining my mother's birth certificate, I truly understood that I had two parents from different races and different places. Momma had an American re-issued birth certificate; the islands had only been purchased eight years prior. The references in Momma's birth certificate were culturally Danish. Granny Sabino was listed as her mother, and Granny 's race was labeled "mixed." I asked myself why the Danish referred to my grandmother as mixed. My eyes scanned across the certificate to the word "mixed" on the maternal side of the page, and to the word "Filipino" on the paternal side of the certificate. I stared at the racial box for baby Norma, but there was no concluding note. I decided to get a history lesson from several of Momma's USVI history books to solve the latest riddle.

Every good island home has, at least, Isaac Dookhan's "*A History of the Virgin Island of the United States,*" or J. Antonio Jarvis', "*The Virgin Islands And Their People*" on their bookshelf. I read them both. Momma's books dropped her story in place. The Virgin Islands historical timeline from 1493-1917 connects dots to such a unique racial scenario for me personally. It simply starts with Christopher Columbus discovering the islands in 1493 on his second New World voyage. He was looking to visit the Carib Islands. The Danish, along with the English, the French and a Diaspora of Jews wanted to colonize the unpopulated island while there were Indians still living there. The Archaic, Taino, and the Carib Indians were the original Virgin Island Amerindian inhabitants along with the Arawak Indians. The Carib Indians fought Columbus off the island at his first appearance. The Spanish and Norwegians have held interests in developing the islands during the 17th, 18th and 19th centuries. The Danish West India Company settled in St. Thomas in 1672, and the islands became the royal Danish colonies in 1754. They developed sugar cane and cotton plantations with slave labor. Slave trade and cargo advanced as industry, so did pirating. The emancipation of slavery in 1848 left the region without a labor force, so the Danish economy in the islands began to suffer. When the 1867 treaty to sell St. Thomas as a coaling station and was finally actualized in 1916; the Danes cut their losses. The United States expressed an interest in purchasing the islands to prevent the Germans from using them as submarine bases during WWI.

Amelia Amanda Collins Sabino was of Irish and Danish West Afro-Caribbean racial admixtures. Our European surname, Collins, tells the story of our Irish Boston merchant forefather. I suspect he was possibly a slave trader. His son, Charles Collins, my great-great-grandfather, born in St. Bartholomew, was a ship rigger in

St. Thomas. He was married to Amelia Heyliger-Pereira Collins born in St. Thomas and descendant from the Dutch island of St. Eustatius. Their son Edward Henley was Granny Sabino's father. Edward connected with my St. John West African Ghanaian descendant maternal great grandmother Fredericka Malvena Collins. Our family called her Bada. As a result, their daughter, my Granny Sabino was considered as a mixed-race, "whitey-clear" island woman. I had to agree with Momma's birth certificate. Granny Sabino and her siblings were such a curious crew of "mixed" folk. Granny prided herself on thinking that she looked like Rose Kennedy, and she sort of did. Granny Sabino and her immediate siblings had a dusty, bright yellow coloring, and she had one very dark-skinned sister, suggesting different fathers. They all had my maternal great-grandmother in common as their mother.

Granny's people had this strange hair that was the texture of cotton candy. My hair isn't too different from theirs. They all had this unusual stuttering, sputtering of their first words spoken. My medium-framed island grandmother kept the island tourists guessing as to what to make of her race as she walked up and down the duty-free alleyways and alcoves of Charlotte Amalie.

Momma's birth certificate was accompanied by baby pictures, family pictures, and Kodak moments canvassing the beautiful geography of island beach scenes and mountain tops. None of the pictures could compare to the fractal frames and pictures of Sinforoso and my mysterious great-grandfather Edward Henley Collins and his grandfather, one Captain Charles Collins from Boston. The living room cocktail table contents remained full of photos along with her folded paper explaining the family tree. It all demanded my attention, immediately.

In Momma's photo album, there was a picture of Momma boarding a Pan-Am flight to America. I have since found the exact Pan-Am manifesto matching Momma's flight to the mainland United States. Momma cleared immigration through San Juan, Puerto Rico in 1946 racially marked as a white woman. Granny wanted Momma to marry a white man because she didn't believe a black man in 1946 could take care of her, so she probably told her to mark her race as "white."

The tragedy of our family's loss was still bitter, and the old house remained as an old scar. The contents of my parent's basement was evidence of that scar, though it is no longer painful. The house was our dad's signature piece. I don't know how he did it, but upon his death at age 44, his estate took care of Momma, our college tuitions, cars, a nice home, and my wedding. Momma fulfilled her dream of becoming a registered nurse and having a family and died in 2000 as a black woman. She got what she came for.

Poppa started biographical files on my brother and me. In The Green Box, we each had a folder packed with our childhood records: photos, report cards, baptismal certificates, awards, kudos, newspaper articles, bills, and receipts. The Green Box was void of any personal references to Poppa, at all. Stashed in Momma's attic was a cardboard box. It was delivered to Momma a few days after Poppa's funeral, and I remembered the day it was delivered to our home. Momma packed it away for my brother to have at a time such as this. On the day of The Green Box discoveries, we found and opened the box to discover all of Poppa's government and career correspondence. Poppa always had that plan for reaching the mayoral office. He'd saved every note documenting his rise to the top. Poppa's career documents spoke of an incredible vision for himself, for us, and for Washington, D.C. Combined in the right order, Poppa's letters told the story of a true black hero.

"You have no idea what your father did for D.C.," Poppa's remaining colleagues and peers remind us. Poor Baby Brother hears this continually while running into Poppa's friends and associates about town. Chico is humbled by their acknowledgements, though they are a painful reminder of what could have been. The Green Box was void of Poppa's personal family secrets, and for the purposes of researching, the scholar in me would soon have to shine. His personal records missing spoke volumes.

Chico had organized everything for cleaning and taking inventory. We closed The Green Box, locked it, and returned it to the back of the basement. We secured the necessary files for conducting our business affairs, but The Green Box had found me. That was God's mission, and he'd been guiding me from the start.

"Let's go eat more crab cakes," I said.

Chico and I finished cleaning out the house that day carrying the discoveries of The Green Box in our hearts and, in my case, in the trunk of my car. During the summer, I brought The Green Box's important files back to New England for research. It became very clear that my own mid-life identity crisis and subsequent sabbatical had everything to do with needing the time necessary to examine The Green Box files. Truth was demanding my attention.

Poppa's Washington, D.C. was changing as history was being made within it. By winter, it was time for Barak Obama's inauguration. My own family and I decided to visit the D.C.'s Mall area weeks before for the Presidential inauguration. Honestly, we'd witnessed so many inaugural events from afar that not even Obama's inauguration was that special anymore. We were going to let the newbies have their fun. When Inauguration Day 2009 did arrive, I was glued to the LD screen. I could only imagine what Poppa would've thought about blacks in the White House. I couldn't help but remember so many defining moments as the Inaugural Parade rolled down Pennsylvania Avenue. In a similar memory, Poppa and I were standing in line at the Capitol on Sunday, November 24th, 1963 when President Kennedy's coffin was carried on a horse-drawn caisson to the U.S. Capitol to lie in state. Poppa held my hand for hours as we waited our turn to approach JFKs flag covered casket. It's a grim memory, but an unforgettable one.

Oh, how the mall and the reflecting pool had changed since my childhood. It was Poppa's favorite backdrop for snapping pictures of Momma. During the Inaugural Parade coverage, CNN clipped video of an interracial couple at the reflection pool and my mind slid back to 1963. I remembered living through The March on Washington where the Reverend Dr. Martin Luther King filled his audience with a dream and a hope of a greater tomorrow. The Lincoln Memorial was his pulpit, and the globe was his altar space. Poppa went to see Dr. Martin Luther King speak; I remained home watching the speech on NBC.

From Dr. Martin Luther King to JFK, from JFK to Obama, the city of my youth had changed. God was forcing me to change right along with it.

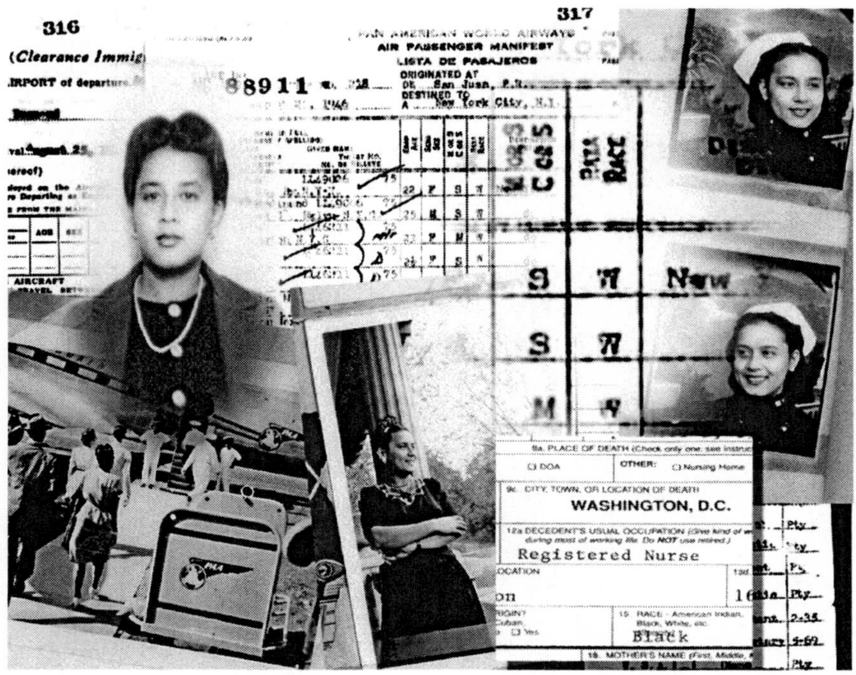

In 1946, Momma came to the United States racially as a white woman. Never having a racial box categorically to fit within, she died as a black woman.

Momma accomplished her life's goal of coming to America for an education, to raise a family and to become a Registered Nurse.

AN ODYSSEY CONCLUDES 2009

It took 16 years for God to put all of the pieces to one heck of a puzzle in my hands. The task before me was daunting, to be sure, but exciting. I began by categorizing all of Momma's photos with the goal of photo finishing and framing my favorites. One of my favorite photos was a Kodak Moment I had never seen.

Ed, our Northwest 19th street apartment friend, was our family photographer. He had taken pictures at Momma's baby shower. Based on the date marked on the back of the photo, I was thirty days from birth when the photo was taken. The black and white 8x10 photo was high-quality and finished on the best of fiber-like Kodak professional photo finishing paper. It didn't look a day over a half-century old. When I discovered the baby shower photo in The Green Box, I purchased a frame for it, and it became my favorite picture from the entire batch. I sat it on the credenza adjacent to my desk. The picture inspired me, as though it was telling me that I was truly my mother's child.

"I am now a believer in your crazy project," Chico said during a midday call in spring 2009. I was driving about New England, and Chico's shrill tone of disbelief almost unnerved me.

"Hey, what's up?" I replied.

"I got this email from a museum consultant. She said that she is working on a project for the Washington Historical Society. Dot, Ed's wife, donated his portfolio to the museum. Guess what?"

"What?"

"She says the collection has pictures of this beautiful woman and a set of baby pictures. The name 'Horace Holmes' is on the back of the pictures. She wants to know if they are my baby pictures because my name is Horace Holmes."

"Well, given the dates, I think they are *my* baby pictures. You weren't born yet."

"Cheryl, she asked me if Momma was a model or something."

"Your mother looks like a movie star," say people who see pictures of my mother in her prime. I was able to put my mother's race drama into perspective when a Filipina Facebook friend on the other side of the world wrote me: "you are blessed with good looks...your mom resembles the Philippine movie actress, Liezl Sumilang, daughter of Amalia Fuentes and Romeo Vasquez... you are so cute..." I put the search term "Philippine Actresses Old and New" into Google and found tons of Momma look-a-likes. Fair-skinned mestizas Filipinas are popular draws for Philippine box offices. Momma was an American nurse who might have been a movie star if she remained in the country of her racial origin.

On my birthday, I traveled to Washington to identify the baby shower photos as well as the other photos in the collection. I found the original negatives and the baby shower pictures preserved in the special collections section of the museum's library. It drove me into studying Momma's record of live birth more closely. I dug into the framework of my family unit by obtaining the 1930 U.S. Census for the U.S. Virgin Islands. There it was, my clue to why the Danish referred to Granny Sabino as "mixed." Granny Sabino's entire family unit, with the exception of my maternal great-great-grandmother, was marked "M." Bada was marked "Negro."

I kept researching, going so far as to have several personal conversations with Dr. David M. Pemberton, an historian with the U.S. Census Bureau. He interpreted the 1930 enumeration guidelines and instructions for me and wrote his findings in a letter to me:

Dear Reverend Miller,

Thank you for your telephone call earlier today asking about the instructions to enumerators about racial classification in the 1930 census in the U.S. Virgin Islands. You indicated that your mother was born to a Filipino man and an Afro-Caribbean/Danish woman in 1923 and that your mother was recorded as a six year-old girl with the racial designation, "M." The 1930 manual of instructions to enumerators stated:

"Any mixture of white and non-white should be reported according to the non-white parent. Mixtures of colored races should be reported according to the race of the father, except Negro-Indian...both black and mulatto persons

are to be returned as Negroes, without distinction. A person of mixed Indian and Negro blood should be returned a Negro, unless the Indian blood predominates and the status as an Indian is generally accepted in the community."

These instructions seem to indicate that your mother should have been classified as being of the same race as her father, i.e., Filipino. The classification "M" does not appear as a race category in the 1930 mainland instructions.

In 1930, on the U.S. mainline, any mixture of White and some other race was to be reported according to the race of the parent who was not white. Mixtures of colored races were to be listed according to the father's race, except Negro-Indian. In this case, race was identified by paternity. By digging a little deeper, I discovered the actual 1930 U.S. Virgin Island Census final bulletin. It is very unclear what my family would have been enumerated as — "other colored," which includes Hindus, Chinese, Filipinos and Indians or as natives of mixed parentage. Nonetheless, by 1940 as race was identified in my family's particular scenario, mixtures of colored races were reported by the paternity. Momma's father was Filipino. Momma died without knowing that the U.S. government should have recognized her as a Philippine-American, the race of her father. Almost all of my mother's immediate maternal family could've been classified as Philippine-American. We'd become racially lost in the pepper sauce and had not even realized it.

St. Eustatius is an island of great wealth. The Dutch forever seized control in the early 19th century. St. Eustatius, as a region of the Netherlands Antilles, was the first country to recognize the independence of the United States on November 16, 1776. The "First Salute" is the first international gun salute acknowledging independence of the American colonies. By 1864, approximately 1,700 immigrants from Barbados and St. Eustatius arrived in St. Thomas as the 1863 emancipation of slave labor drove mercantile endeavors north. The merchants on St. Eustatius provided much of the arms, gunpowder and ammunition used by the rebels in the American Revolution. St. Eustatius was colonized by the Zeeland Chamber of the Dutch West India Company. The Heyliger family in the West Indies were among the first settlers on the island in 1636. The Heyligers are known as governors throughout the course of the islands' history. Granny's paternal great grandmother was a Heyliger proper or possibly a Heyliger free mulatto. She raised her own children and grandchildren in the Dutch Reform Church in St. Thomas.

Granny Sabino was regarded a mulatto on one of the most complete transfer intakes recorded in the 1930 U.S. Census for the USVI. The 1917 U.S. census first identified island residents as part of the transitional sale; it is also known as the 1920 U.S. census for the islands. Thus, Granny Sabino was marked "mixed" on my mother's birth certificate, though there was more to it than that. As mentioned, Granny 's paternal great grandmother was from St.

Eustatius-Dutch West Indies; her daughter Amelia Pereira married Charles Collins. These were Granny's grandparents. They gave birth to Granny Sabino's father, Edward, in 1865/6. Son, Edward, found his way to Granny's mother, Bada, who was from the St. John-Danish West Indies. Bada's family has West African heritage from the Ga Tribe and the African slaves who revolted during the 1733 Coral Bay Slave Insurrection. My Danish West African lineage is from the Ga People, who fought the Akwamu Tribe.

Specifically, many of my Sowah tribal family members were sold into slavery by the Danes, and shipped from Christianborg Castle dungeons in OSU, Ghana, and brought to plantations in the West Indies. Some of these plantations were located in St. John, specifically the Coral Bay regions.

My "whitey" mixed-race grandmother is the carrier of my West African DNA. In 1900, the Danish were fighting to survive their failing colonization plans. Since they were making no gain with colonizing the islands, Denmark wanted out. The United States wanted the territory as a central coaling spot and as a military water access point similar to the Panama Canal. A Danish-translated 1880 St. John census record exhibited four maternal great-grandmothers of mine all enumerated in one family unit. Bada was 6 years old.

Virgin Islanders have been gathering on Facebook to share USVI culture, memories, history, family stories, recipes, travel tips and more. Sharing vintage postcards is a popular trend with members of the USVI Facebook fan page. I found Danish West Indian antique postcards from late 1800s and early 1900s, but the most interesting item I found was my USVI maternal cousin, Larry Sewer.

Larry and I reviewed our Danish West Indian slave history, the facts of the 1733 St. John slave insurrection at Coral Bay, our St. John Family tree, and island oral traditions. Larry is the first Sewer family member to have returned to Ghana to meet his Ghanaian family as well as his Ga-Sowah tribal family. Bada's name was Fredericka Malvena Dougherty (Sewer) Collins. She was the daughter of Romeo Dougherty and Amanda Sewer Robles, half sister of the acclaimed Amsterdam News sports editor, Romeo L. Dougherty and granddaughter to St. John's 19th century fisherman and carpenter, Martin Sewer, Sr. of Coral Bay. The Sewer-Dougherty surnames are indigenous families to Coral Bay and are of Danish West African-Ga descent. They remain a people of the harbor. From his research and journeys, Cousin Larry had compiled a tremendous amount of oral tradition and Ghanaian history. He sent me quite the informative message:

"There is the river called Last Bath. Our families from Cameroon, Togo, and adjoining areas had their last bath here before their long journey to Cape Coast. There, the males and females who resisted were placed in dungeons. The women who were hosed down were for the pleasure of the magistrates and, later, the soldiers. The Cape Coast is where I screamed so loud that Heaven heard my cry."

Knowing my family's Danish West African surname and tribal origins gave me a remarkable feeling of peace. Lawdy, here was another cousin introducing me to my family via Kodak Moments. All of this Middle Passage history collided with Sinforoso landing in St. Thomas.

The Green Box file folder marked "Cheryl" brought to mind painful memories of the race war in my home. Poppa kept all of my records in that folder, and as I read them I had vivid memories of his love for me. Upon Chico's birth, Poppa had started a folder for him, too. The Green Box file folders had all of my report cards from two elementary schools, each one indicating a bright future in academics. I remembered the mornings that Momma walked me to school. My folder was so full of memories both fond and painful.

There were newspaper clippings of winning my first art contests, little drawings for school newsletters, a handwritten letter to Aunt Mary for her joke collection, and lots of photo negatives from Ed's dark room. The folder brought to life everything I went through in my childhood with my crazy mixed up family—even the picture of me in a red dress. I hated that dress. I'd found priceless information in The Green Box, and it wasn't finished with me yet.

There was a reason why Poppa had no personal photographs, photo albums or personal family artifacts about, and I hadn't processed all of the photo negatives.

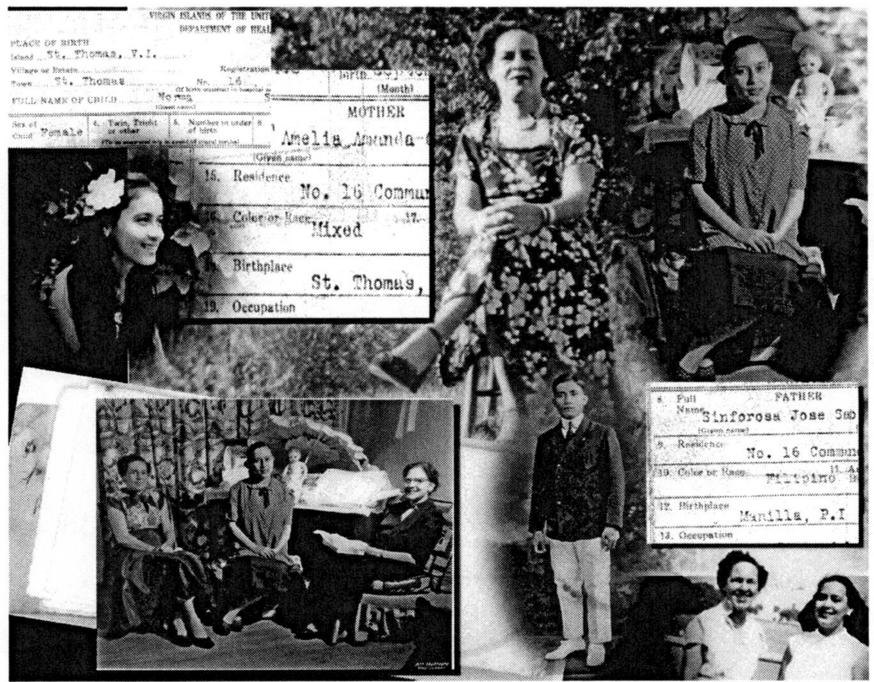

A misinterpreted U.S. census enumeration guideline denied our family rights to be regarded as Philippine Americans as well as ethnically West Indian. My maternal grandmother was regarded as mixed on my mother's birth certificate and Momma's father was noted as Filipino. My maternal family has self-identified racially in America by any means necessary.

Center: Amelia Collins Sabino, my island Granny Sabino and Momma.

"Baby Brother, I took those negatives to the shop for processing," I said to my brother during a call. "I opened the envelope and nearly fainted in the store. I couldn't believe my eyes. I have never seen these pictures, and never knew Ed took this particular photograph. It is a generational shot of Pops, Poppa, and you. You are about 2 months old or so; it's obviously your Christening Day. My God, Baby Brother, what a photo. Pops looks so much like a white man, Poppa looks as we remember him, and you are sitting on his knee looking like a little Asian baby."

The picture was and is like a gem to me. I purchased another frame, later placing it next to Momma's baby shower picture. The Green Box negative had come to life and was now haunting me to uncover yet another family mystery. The answer was stashed away in the cardboard box on the top of my closet. The Green Box negative drew me back to the beginning of this entire odyssey. It was the anonymously-written document filed in the first cardboard box that shed light on more of my family secrets. Opening the door to my Ancestry.com account confirmed all of the document's records as accurate. I discovered Eleanor Gaines, Elvira Gaines, and Hester Gaines as descendant grandmothers of my paternal grandfather, Pops.

I had Chico send his DNA to familytreedna.com because I wanted to know where I got my Caucasian admixture from on my father's side of the family. As a result, Chico and I received many "pings" from The William Strother Society. The William Strother

Society's purpose is to discover the origins of 1800's immigrant William Strother. The primary question surrounding Strother is if he originated from England or Scotland. I had Chico send his DNA to familytreedna.com; the William Strother Society was also testing male samples. We were shocked to find out that Chico was a DNA match to William Strother. Many modern mulatto Southerners have a racial root somewhere in their DNA of an early American immigrant. The British Isle Immigrant, William Strother, settled in colonial Virginia, where he was given a southern land grant upon arrival to America. The Strothers themselves were indigenous to what is now King George County, VA on the Rappahannock River near Port Conway. Specifically, my paternal European Y-DNA of origin is from William Strother. American presidents Jimmy Carter and Zachary Taylor are also William Strother match-descendants. My brother's paternal Y-DNA markers are registered to my Family Tree DNA Worldwide account. Prominent William Strother Society members continue to match my account as genetic cousins.

Altogether, I met several paternal Gaines Holmes-descendant cousins who have been researching our paternal families. We've compared notes and continue to check in with each other when new findings surface. Cousin Marlene would be the one to tie everything together. I went to Pittsburgh for a 48-hour stay with Marlene when the Mid-Atlantic was free of its winter storms. Marlene and I, having embarked on the same quest, shared our combined knowledge, photos, and documents.

"Marlene, how come I didn't know my family," I asked her. There was one picture of Sadie in the midst of her family photo albums.

"Marlene, there is only one picture of Sadie, and only one or two photos of me. What do you make of it?"

"Sadie didn't want her photo taken much, Cheryl," Marlene said with certainty.

"We thought your father left the family."

"Marlene, how do you leave a family?"

I knew the answer. You cut off anything that might harm the children, even if it's family.

As I discovered through our combined research, it turned out that my paternal great grandparents, George and Mollie, were actually uncle and niece. My collective Gaines-descent grandmothers galloped across Antebellum Virginia, having begun an incredible white and Amerindian inter-marrying clan that mixed and matched with black folks along the way. They made and raised families and all of their progeny looked like white people. Poppa didn't want this clannish behavior anywhere near his wife, his daughter, his son, or his career. They would've never accepted Momma; she was different from them on a level that not even she could fully comprehend.

With our time for sharing coming to a close, Marlene pulled out the *pièce_de_résistance* by showing me an original photographic portrait of Hester Gaines, a pure Amerindian woman. In the adjacent photograph, there was a well-preserved picture of Pops' mother and his two sisters as small children. They were clearly a breed of white and Amerindian people who made a beautiful family amongst the African-American community, regardless of how that family came to be. The final picture Marlene showed me was one of Poppa in his childhood. Poppa and his siblings enjoyed a day at a Chesapeake Bay beach with their Amerindian-plus admixture grandmother, Mollie Timbers Holmes Pearl. I recognized Poppa at age 6, and after examining the photo for a minute or two, I could recognize everyone.

Poppa never left a trace of his family in The Green Box or any other place in the house. Yet, Marlene had countless pictures of Poppa standing with white-lookin' folks I had never seen. Poppa knew of our family members who "passed" for white, and who went in and out of being available for family photos. Poppa had integrated into his Negro mother's family and never mentioned anything of the photo truths. Being light brown, he couldn't associate with any member of his "passin' white" side of the family, and he couldn't take us to places he wasn't allowed to go himself.

We couldn't bond with a family that wasn't always there. For me, the truth had finally come out, and it'd come through reconnecting with my estranged paternal family. After a lifetime of heartache and injury, my family's internal war was truly over. Total enlightenment brought a peace and happiness that caused my black hole to shrink and shrivel until it was no more.

Waiting to board my flight home, I uploaded a few photos to my brother.

"I have a surprise for you," I texted him. I didn't receive a reply from him for days. There was much for him to think about. Since that time, I would like to believe that the bliss which had overcome me at Marlene's would pass on to him. We'd both suffered through the same nightmare. The center of our family's racial tension always seemed to be centered on Momma's Asian mixed bloodedness and West Indian ethnicity. It was all too much for my American family to accept; they had no sensibility toward diversity.

It's hard to imagine that black folks can't accept diversity, but my family was intolerant of its own. Chico and I agreed that while Poppa remained focused on his goals and aspirations, he'd played a part in the family drama. I can only imagine what Momma went through in America amidst all of my paternal family's drama and a daughter who was always wandering in search of a "real" Negro mother. There were two, final items in The Green Box that had significance to me. Poppa had written a letter to the Dean of The Rhode Island School of Design when I first applied there:

> *"Cheryl didn't do as well in high school as I had hoped; a solid student, though– I think she fell in love, a little, with the class president..."*

The other item was a letter that Momma wrote to the Head of the National Cathedral for Girls after I interviewed there. Momma pushed for me to get a scholarship.

"See Cheryl, Momma was thinking about you after all," Baby Brother said at the time we read the letter.

"Yeah," was about all I could grunt. Momma was always thinking about me, and in the basement of the home she raised me in, I was thinking about her.

"Cheryl, be prepared in case Prince Charming doesn't come along," *Poppa* ***admonished. I married Phillip our senior high school class president.***

Poppa was mystery raced himself. Top left: Great, great grandmother Hester Gaines, daughter of Elvira Gaines, Fauquier County, Virginia. Right bottom: The Gaines Clan featuring my great-great grandmother Hester and her daughter, my great grandmother Mollie at her shoulder from Fauquier County, Virginia; Bottom left bottom: Poppa and me as well as Pops.

My Holmes paternal lineage: Top left: Poppa, The Holmes brothers, Bottom left and center: Pops, my great grandmother Mollie with her daughters (Pops' sisters) and one of the best "Green Box" photos: A generational photo of Pops, Poppa and little brother, Chico.

I APOLOGIZE

My story isn't about race. It's about discovering Momma, and finding the family I never had. I can only say one thing to all of them now—

Momma, I'm sorry; forgive me.

Momma, I am so sorry. I love you so much, and I had no idea you had it so hard. I've had it difficult in so many ways, just as you did. Irony.

Poppa, thank you for keeping me focused. I appreciated you for every moment you were in my life.

Dear Lord, I forgive Sadie and Sinforoso. Allow me to forgive all those dead-gone D.C. divas who didn't want Momma's friendship.

Thank you, God, for my U.S. Virgin Island family that bridged the gap as best possible.

Thank you Lisa, for praying Aunt Nannie's prayer to find me, which led me to finding the family I'd never really known.

God, thank you for teaching me that family is the most important thing in life.

Phillip, I will love you always. Chico you will always be dear to me. Amen and amen.

The Revolutionary Hill

While operating my design firm in New York, I worked with some of the best photographers in the industry. On one occasion, I received quite an attractive set of portrait prints from a photographer I worked with. He was thanking me. I thought one particular photo would make a good gift for Phillip's office. I purchased a nice glass frame with an extra thick glass back stand, and then gave him the framed picture.

One evening, Phillip came home with an interesting note about the day's events and business encounters.

"Cheryl, you want to hear something interesting," was his opening line at dinner. On this particular day, he had been visited by an associate from China. "He looked at a picture of you in my office and said 'Maganda', is that your wife? I said 'yes, she is.' He asked if you were Filipina. I asked what 'Maganda' meant. He said it was Filipino for 'beautiful.' I told him my wife's mother is Philippine American, half-Filipina."

I should have suspected that when an Asian gentleman sees the Filipina in me and acknowledges what he recognizes as "Maganda" I needed to accept that my mother's racial ancestry was my own.

"I want to take you to Tokyo, Hong Kong and China for our 25th wedding anniversary," Phillip said. "Cheryl, do you want to go to

Hong Kong? I would love to show you everywhere I have been in Asia. We can start off in Tokyo and end in Beijing."

Phillip couldn't have planned a better time to travel to Asia. The entire region was buzzing with anticipation, preparation and excitement. God would have the blessed coincidence of our trip taking place alongside Bill Clinton's 1998 nine-day state visit to China. Preparation for American tourism was all about the geography. When we went to the Emperor's Temple-Meiji Shrine in Tokyo, my eyes slipped away from Phillip's pseudo-tour guiding.

"Honey, my God— Aw Phillip, is this my imagination? Are those people staring at me? Here we go again, Lawdy..."

"Cheryl, where—who's looking at you? I don't see anyone," Phillip said. I quirked my neck to the right. "Over there Phillip, that little couple is staring at me. Mercy, not again." I perceived that a little Asian couple, a husband and wife team, were getting ready to gang up on me.

"Cheryl, you are right. She's running toward us," Phillip said. Phillip held my hand.

The wife ran up to me and it turns out she could speak English.

"Are you Japanese," she asked.

"No, I am black, African American," I replied. You can't imagine the look on her face, but you can imagine the look on mine.

To my friends, family, and New England community, I'd disappeared from society during my sabbatical. I'd been out of regular church membership for two years. I'd completed my reflective journey, and I wanted to return to full church membership on a gradual basis. I crawled into the nearest church I could find that wasn't a black church, like the ones I'd been serving in for the past 26 years. In our home, on an evening in August 2010, I approached Phillip with my dilemma.

"Phillip, I am worried about the children, they aren't in church. I can understand what is happening to me, but I don't want whatever the Lord is doing with me to impede the kids' growth. I have to admit, I feel safer and more blessed out of church. Lawdy, Phillip, this is so sad."

"Cheryl, I'll just start teaching the children on Sunday mornings," Phillip replied. "We'll have home church. I would worry more if we are in the wrong place with them."

I had lived my life entirely as a black woman, and with whatever time I had left, God required me to face new dreams, aspirations, missions, and accomplishments as a *multi-racial* woman. God needed me to operate in all four corners of my racial ambiguity. From my early days in seminary, I knew that I was called to explore multiculturalism in the church, but never knew how to do that in the black church. I had been fully indoctrinated in the African-American church lifestyle which is a world all its own.

My transition back to church attendance was interesting. "Phillip, I am going to church this morning. I have no idea where I am going," I told Phillip one Sunday morning. "I am going to drive until the Spirit says stop."

"Do you want me to go with you," Phillip asked.

When I was in the black church, I was in it as a black woman and identified myself as such. However, if I wanted things to be different, I was going to have to walk in the truth of a new, multi-racial perspective. Poppa's family had passed for white, I wanted to see what it was like to do that just once in my most familiar environment. I wanted to go to church as a "white woman" as an experiment and didn't want Phillip and the family to come with me. They *insisted* otherwise. We drove until the Spirit told us to stop at the First Right Congregational Anglo New England Protestant Carpenter Gothic Church. I told my family to stay in the car. I didn't want them to come with me in the first place. I compromised my adventure by saying that they could come in with me, but would have to come in after me and act like they didn't know me. I went inside before everyone else and seated myself. Within minutes, my daughter came in.

"Mommie, Mommie," my daughter ran toward me and took a seat next to me.

"Can't you...Aw...forget it. Sit down," I said. "This experiment is OVER before it even started. Next time I won't tell a soul I am leaving the house."

I have been in church nearly my entire adult life. In the pew, in the aisle, around the altar and in the pulpit, I know my way around every corner of the church. I have never had this happen before. While sitting in the pew, my panty hose started slipping off and falling down.

"Are you OK?" Phillip is bending over, and looking down to the end of the row. "What's wrong with you? Why are you squirming in your seat?" "Sssh. I can't believe this, my panty hose are crawling down my legs. I have to get out of this service quickly. If I stand up, these things are going to fall off. I wish the preacher would hurry up and finish," I am between laughing to tears and fearing embarrassment.

The one hour service couldn't move along fast enough. I began looking for the exit sign and signage for the rest rooms. After the benediction, I found my way to the ladies' room. No sooner did I begin my stocking repair, there was a knock on the restroom door.

"Mommie, hurry. Daddy wants you to come to the fellowship hall," my daughter said through the door.

"What does he want, dear God? Give me a minute, I will be right there," I replied.

I joined Phillip's conversation with a white woman. "Belinda, this is my wife Cheryl; Cheryl, this is Belinda," Phillip said. "Cheryl, Belinda asked me a question which I felt you could best answer for yourself."

"Sure," I replied with a question mark plastered on my face.

"Mrs. Miller, are you Filipina?," Belinda dared to ask.

"Why do you ask? Before I respond, I'd like to know what would make you think I am Filipina?"

"When I saw you enter the sanctuary, I immediately thought you to be Filipina. I lived in Manila for four years after my husband's job relocated us there for an assignment.

The minute you came into the church, I noticed you look like the women of Manila. I love everything about the Philippines, and I just wanted to connect with you."

"Yes, I am mixed Filipina, of Filipino descent—from my Mom." I was speechless as it was the very first time I claimed my mother's racial heritage.

So many of my life's occasions had been screaming of my Philippine heritage and descent. My MIA Sabino Philippine family is from Cavite and the neighboring areas of Manila Bay. Although they have not been a part of my life, it doesn't mean I am not of Philippine descent. If I look like the women of Manila, there is a reason. My unknown SABINO family is from Manila and the surrounding townships.

Around the corner from my home is a white Carpenter Gothic clapboard Protestant Congregational Church that is smaller than the one I experimented with. On a near-autumn Sunday, I entered the church, grabbed their bulletin and claimed a front row seat.

I was filled with the expectancy of fall's first Sunday morning approaching and was intrigued by this small, attractive church. I read that Sunday's bulletin:

"Disillusionment is the loss of illusion–about ourselves, about the world, about God–and while it is almost always painful, it is not a bad thing to lose the lies we have mistaken for truth. Disillusioned, we come to understand that God does not conform to our expectations. Disillusioned, we find out what is not true and are set free to seek what is–if we dare."
Barbara Brown Taylor

Since I had never expected to ever be in a little New England church worshipping with white folks, I was most definitely in foreign territory, but I knew God was at work. I'd been traveling disillusionment's highway straight to the open doors of this little church where I could start over. I continued reading the bulletin. The entire liturgy and litany pointed to its central theme of spiritual renewal and revival–just what it means to be a clay vessel in the Potter's Hands. I made an appointment to speak to the pastor, since I wanted to know more about the quote.

"Reverend Miller, the quote is from the book *Leaving The Church* by the Episcopal priest and theologian Barbara Brown Taylor. She is a Yale Divinity graduate and a former Episcopal priest.

You might enjoy all of her writings. I just adore her sermons," Reverend Diane, the pastor of this unique church, told me during a conversation in her office.

"Her quote speaks more than volumes to what has happened to me," I said. "If it's alright, I'd like my fellowship here kept quiet until the Lord speaks to my heart and shows me what's next. I really need to park my family somewhere safe while I'm in spiritual rehab. I pray that God tells me if I am to continue in ministry or retire."

"Reverend Miller, you are more than welcome to fellowship with us. Bring your family."

I brought the kids to the church's Easter service. Afterwards, my children participated in a few festivities and worship services. As 2010 ended, I spent my 58th birthday discovering more about the American Revolution legacy of church life and signs that I should return to ministry.

Outside of the church, the local Jack and Jill Holiday Luncheon has become my favorite Christmas tradition. Every year, my son prepares a vocal selection for the luncheon, and my daughter offers a dance or drama contribution. I look forward to these precious moments.

My son's voice school has a recital every holiday season, and he uses that recital to rehearse for the Jack and Jill Holiday luncheon. After Christmas 2010's recital, the family was hungry.

"Let's go for Chinese," my son suggested. His sister and father agreed. I shook my head.

"Are you people in your right mind? Chinese food at 10 o'clock at night?"

We ventured to our favorite Chinese bistro. I ate the last dumpling knowing I would face lots of trouble for eating it that late in the evening. The pain it gave me at 2 a.m. forced Phillip to call an ambulance fearing that I was having a heart attack.

"Reverend Miller, you didn't have a heart attack," a surgeon told me. "You have a very large gallstone and one very large kidney stone. They have to be removed immediately. I'm amazed they haven't bothered you at all given your age."

I had a successful surgery. Reverend Diane called me from the hospital.

"I'm fine, Pastor. I am fine. I will be out in a few days," I told Reverend Diane.

"I called to check on you and to tell you something very important. I am not renewing my contract with the church because I'd like to spend more time with my family. I will be reassigned soon, and I'm not concerned about it."

"Well...Pastor, we will pray and trust it will be well," I said, closing the conversation with a gulp. A few days passed, and Reverend Diane called again to check on me.

"Reverend Miller, how are you? Before you answer, I have something to share. The musician at the church resigned," Reverend Diane said. "Connect The Dots" is an easy game; I could see the highway clear and straight ahead. I was soon standing before the search committee and interviewing for Reverend Diane's vacant position. Not long after that, I was informed of the affirmative vote to make me the new pastor.

When I entered back into ministry, I began to think about how my journey had reframed me for this new assignment. I knew exactly how to answer the questions "what are you" and "where are you from" before they could be asked. To make my new office more welcome for visitors, I brought all of my discovered photo fractals and photographs of my family out into the open. I put them all into new frames and gave each one a spot on my book shelves. Sorry, Grandmother Sadie didn't make my office shelf.

I am just a minister. I'm not perfect by any means.

I was creating new space for self-identifying in a new way as a clergywoman. After countless interviews, records, and pictures finding their way to me, I wanted more. I wanted to know what Momma thought of her situation before she started squeezing in this American "one drop" drama, so I dared to call Howard University for her college application records. I received a copy of my father's records, as well.

"Dr. Miller, I see your mother's race was 'mixed.' I see from your Dad's records, he was a really smart guy. He had a B+ average for his entire time in school," the Howard University records officer said. Momma filled in the race box on her college application as "mixed."

All of Momma's records, from her 1952 baby shower to her death certificate melded into a single realization: Granny Sabino was mixed and Momma was mixed, so I couldn't be anything but Norma Sabino's mixed-race baby girl.

"Reverend Miller, you have such an interesting story and family photos," a congregant said when they stopped by my office to welcome me to the church.

"They are all here now, out of the photo albums and out of the box. This is the first time my family has something in common. They're resting peacefully on my book case together, finally they are getting along," I replied.

"Reverend, the 2010 Census records for our state and city have been published. The white population declined 3% percent, the black population has declined 5%, and the Hispanic community is the largest minority group in our city. The Asian population is the fastest growing population at 65%. You are a perfect fit for our church and community. Your story is so amazing, but what are
you, Reverend?"

I paused, and then smiled. "A child of God."

For the first time in my life, my family is getting along peacefully, on the bookshelves of my pastoral office. When visitors come to visit, the "What Are You? Where Are You From? " perplexing stare has vanished. It's pretty clear; my photos tell our family's incredible story.

EPILOGUE

Locating my family has been like finding Black Coral. Black Coral lies deep within the coral gardens of the tropical deep waters and sea. It is exotic and rare, most precious in color above all other varieties, and often threatened by harvesters wanting to exploit it. Black Coral is often found embedded within the warm waters of the Philippines, the Caribbean and Africa–Black Coral grows in caves under ledges where light is dim; it thrives in the darkness. It grows like trees up from the ocean floor and is as hard as ivory and pearl. If discovered, Black Coral is adorned with diamonds and gold–like that which was hidden and now becomes clearly seen– as the Glory of God for those who yet wait and still believe. Black Coral, in Latin, is "antipathes subpinnata." It means "against suffering."

My Facebook profile account is full of every Sabino friend I can "friend." On Facebook, I'm always asking, seeking "Do you know my grandfather?" or "Are you my family?"

My grandmother searched for Sinforoso, my mother searched for Sinforoso, and now I've taken up the cause. A 'Sabino' Google search engine led me to the LinkedIn profile page of Pastor Jon Sabino. I wrote to him, and he replied:

Dear Rev. Dr. Cheryl,

This is Pastor Jon Sabino and I work here in Bacoor Evangelical School. If you could give me some information regarding Sinforoso Jose Sabino, i.e., where he lived in Cavite or anything related to him–where he worked here etc., I would gladly make a search for your Sabino Family here in Cavite. Where are you in the U.S.? I'll be flying to the U.S. this October. So we might meet if you want. I can send any information ASAP as I gather it. Hoping for your reply.
Ptr. Jon Sabino

In the fall 2011, I went to Jersey City, NJ to meet Pastor Jon Sabino at a Filipino buffet. We connected through the Internet, and as his last name indicates, he is part of Momma's distant Philippine island family. It has brought me great joy to be able to meet Pastor Jon and all of my other family members I couldn't meet in my youth. Pastor Jon's first stop in the mainland U.S. was California, where he gathered oral tradition from our family historians on the West Coast. I held my breath as he approached me in the restaurant.

"Bishop Miller, your grandfather, Sinforoso Jose Sabino...we know him as 'Lolo Pon Choing,' " Pastor Jon said in a slow, sultry tone. He paused a moment or two before continuing. " 'Lolo Pon Choing' is his nickname. My great-grandfather is his first cousin." "Their fathers were brothers. I will introduce you to our family historian, Gener.

He will share more. Pastor Miller, I had only put up my LinkedIn page a few days prior to you discovering it."

My family outnumbers the grains of sand on a St. Thomas, Virgin Island beach.

My Filipino family from Cavite, Philippines arrived in America. They had a lot to explain to me and my brother. The End, for now.

ABOUT THE AUTHOR

C.D. Holmes Miller

The Rt. Reverend Dr. Cheryl D. Holmes-Miller aka Bishop CD Miller, M.S., MDiv., is a Clergywoman, Theologian, Communications Designer and author. She is the Senior Minister of The North Stamford Congregational Church, Stamford Connecticut. Her church established during the American Revolution is also best known for embracing diversity as the 1957 home church of The Jackie Robinson Family. She has a dual status as an ordained minister for The United Church of Christ and The American Baptist Churches, USA in service to denominational local parishes.

She was consecrated to the bishopric by the Holy Light Pentecostal Ministries, Inc. for her service to worldwide missions.

She is a Master of Divinity graduate of the Union Theological Seminary in New York City and a Benjamin E. Mays scholar. She holds the Master of Science-Communications Design degree from the

Pratt Institute, N.Y. and the Bachelor of Fine Arts from the Maryland Institute College of Art. She is a former business owner; Cheryl D. Miller Design, Inc., New York serviced corporate communications to a Fortune 500 clientele. She has received numerous Honorary Doctorate degrees for her service to the Gospel Ministry.

Notoriety is a part of her legacy. She has countless design industry awards and feature magazine appearances. Gospel Ministry awards and citations follow Reverend Miller's contributions.

Multiracial and multiethnic of Philippine American and African American descent, her families are found in the Americas, The U.S. Virgin Islands and Cavite, Philippines. Bishop C.D. Miller Ministries, LLC. is recognized for Women in Ministry advocacy, globally.

She has traveled and ministers globally throughout Europe, Asia, The Mediterranean, Africa and the Caribbean Islands. C.D Holmes Miller is uniquely a multiracial, multiethnic author with a worldwide voice. She speaks a 21st century message of healing, revival and reconciliation to the nations; it all begins with embracing one's true identity, love of God, self and family.

MOMMA'S RECIPES

Mommy's Favorite: Mrs. Miller's Macaroni & Cheese~page 17.

For macaroni and cheese you will need:

2 sticks of REAL BUTTER, sliced into thin, about 1/8" or ¼" pats

2 16oz, boxes of elbow macaroni

salt and pepper

4 cups of shredded cheddar cheese

8 eggs

4 cups of whole milk

bread crumbs

Now you need a lasagna size casserole pan. The corning ware or Pyrex glass or aluminum pan type, 13 x 9 x 3 - extra deep.

Directions:

1. Rinse the pan and dry to prepare.

We will be LAYERING the ingredients; this is the secret it's in the layers.

2. First layer slice pats of butter and line patty squares around the bottom of the pan, not too many and just enough.

3. Then lay/place on top the butter a layer of cooked elbows.

4. This is a very important step. Sprinkle salt and pepper over this layer.

5. Now repeat a layer of butter patties on top of the elbows.

6. Now toss the cheese over this layer across and to the edge of the pan...completely cover one layer of cheese over the elbows.

So you have:

a layer of butter to line the pan

a layer of elbows

a layer of butter patties

a layer of sprinkled salt and pepper

a layer of cheese

7. Repeat all layers again starting with a layer of elbows until you reach the top of the pan comfortable to hold the liquid

So you will now have:

a layer of elbows

a layer of butter patties

a layer of sprinkled salt and pepper

a layer of cheese

8. Depending on the depth of the pan keep making the pattern of complete layers over and over until you reach near the top of your casserole dish. You have to leave space for bubbling while baking. Filling it to the top will make it spill over and burn.

9. Take eight eggs and 4 cups of milk and blend together. Mix, stir or blend however until it looks like the color of rich egg nog or a custard. Add more eggs if needed in order to have a custard color.

10. Now carefully poor over the layers filling the casserole nearly to the top with the liquid. Leave room for the bubbling while cooking. I line the bottom of my oven with aluminum foil just in case of the bubbling over and spilling. It will smoke up your oven so be careful. Don't fill everything to the tippy top of the pan and you will be fine.

11. Now sprinkle bread crumbs over the top of the entire casserole.

12. Bake at 400 or 425 degrees in the oven for about 45 minutes to an hour and a half. The length of cooking time all depends on your oven i.e. how hot and fast it cooks. Bake in casserole covered with aluminum foil and then uncovered the last 30 minutes.

13. At 45 minutes check and see how it is cooking. If the top browns to a golden color before finishing cover with the casserole top or aluminum foil. Bake it covered the rest of the way. Don't let the top burn now. So start watching around 40 minutes into the baking process.

14. Keep checking until everything is firm. This is the important part and depends on prayer. You have to judge when it's finished. Slow and steady, have patience until it is finished and it will be perfect.

You can substitute fat free dairy items to make a light version. If you want a real hit parade, make the fully leaded version. Makes great left overs and I freeze squares for quick microwaving.

Mommy's Cod Fish Cakes and Pepper Sauce Recipe~page 42.

For Pepper Sauce In A Bottle, you will need:

A clear bottle the size of a standard ketchup or olive oil bottle

A variety of hot peppers and all colors

Fresh: Garlic, Onion, Thyme, Bay Leaf, Fresh Cloves Allspice, Mint, White Vinegar and Olive Oil

Directions, this was Mommy's favorite condiment; a must in an island home:

Slice all the peppers in small (not tiny) pieces and put in bottle. Fill the bottle with all of the fresh spices~no special amount of each. Now pour over ingredients and fill bottle with three quarters white vinegar and one quarter olive oil.

Put on kitchen table and just let it simmer. Use sparingly; it gets hot over time just brewing on your table or shelf.

For Cod Fish Cakes aka Saltfish Fritters, you will need:

1/4 lb dried and salted codfish

1 medium sized onion

4 cloves of garlic

1 medium sized green pepper

A few scallions and hot peppers to taste

2 ripe red medium sized tomatoes

1/4 lb flour

1/2 tablespoon of paprika

Directions:

Soak the codfish in water overnight so as to extract the extra salt. The salt fish is white and hard as a rock. The salt fish is formed in thin sandwich sized flat blocks and packaged in clear plastic wrap.

After soaking the fish over night and in the morning, boil the codfish for about 20 minutes to remove any leftover salt and salty taste. Remove the fish from its soaking water, and shred the fish finely into flakes. Set aside. Now combine the onions, garlic, scallions, green and hot peppers and tomatoes all together into a spicy ingredient type compose. Heat oil in advance.

Fry the seasonings separately and then set them aside. Fold the prepared codfish into a shiny steel cooled mixing bowl; mix the flour into the fish and then slowly added cold water to make a thin batter. Take the previously set aside fried seasonings and now add the paprika; then mix it all together to complete the batter.

Drop the batter down into the sizzling hot oil, a spoonful at a time. Pan fry to a golden brown crisp on both sides, and drain the cakes on paper towels until it was time for serving. The best part of it all for Momma was bringing her pepper sauce brew to the table while giving us her mischievous lil' smile, "Voila, ma'an."

My Family Tree

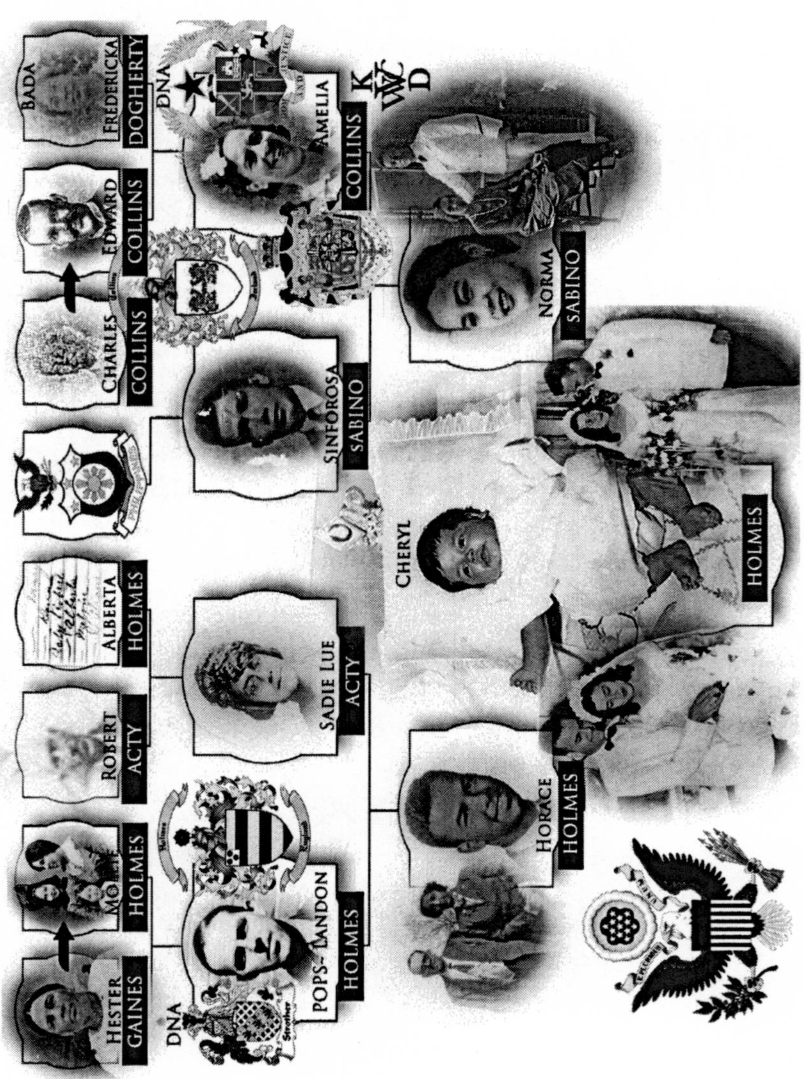

Reverend Miller, we would like to have you speak and share your story in light of the current trending topics:

□ Diversity and Multicultural Awareness □ Genealogy □ Mixed Race Studies □ Asian American Studies □ African American Studies □ Ethnic Biographies □ Caribbean Studies □ Women In Ministry □ Blended Families □ The 21st Century Church □ Visiting Our Book Club □ Gospel Ministry Topical Studies □ Information for ordering more books □ Just to say Thank You For Sharing Your Story, Black Coral, With Us. *Mail Today:*

Name:____

Address:______________________________________

City:____

Postal Code:__________ State or Province:____________

Email:____

Fax:____

Phone:____

Aage Heritage Press~1127 High Ridge Road #241

Stamford, Connecticut 06903

To Order More Books:

Websites: http://cdholmesmiller.com

http://aageheritagepress.com
http://blackcoralthebook.com

Email: info@cdholmesmiller.com

CPSIA information can be obtained at www.ICGtesting.com
Printed in the USA
LVOW08s1253291013

359074LV00002B/40/P

9 780989 263207